Teaching Gend
School

In a set of compelling letters to teachers, Tara Goldstein addresses a full range of issues facing lesbian, gay, bisexual, transgender, and queer (LGBTQ) students and families at elementary and secondary school. Goldstein talks to teachers about how they can support LGBTQ students and families by normalizing LGBTQ lives in the curriculum, challenging homophobic and transphobic ideas, and building an inclusive school culture that both expects and welcomes LGBTQ students and their families. Moving and energizing, *Teaching Gender and Sexuality at School* provides readers with the knowledge and resources they need to create safer and more positive classrooms and discusses what it takes to build authentic, trusting relationships with LGBTQ students and families. Includes "The Unicorn Glossary" by benjamin lee hicks, the performed ethnography *Snakes and Ladders* by Tara Goldstein, and the verbatim play *Out at School* by Tara Goldstein, Jenny Salisbury, and Pam Baer.

Tara Goldstein is Professor of Education in the Department of Curriculum, Teaching and Learning Ontario Institute for Studies in Education of the University of Toronto.

benjamin lee hicks, Jenny Salisbury, and **Pam Baer** are PhD candidates at the Ontario Institute for Studies in Education, and the Centre for Drama, Performance and Theatre Studies, University of Toronto.

Teaching Gender and Sexuality at School

Letters to Teachers

Tara Goldstein
With contributions by benjamin lee hicks,
Jenny Salisbury, and Pam Baer

Routledge
Taylor & Francis Group
NEW YORK AND LONDON

First published 2019
by Routledge
52 Vanderbilt Avenue, New York, NY 10017

and by Routledge
2 Park Square, Milton Park, Abingdon, Oxon, OX14 4RN

Routledge is an imprint of the Taylor & Francis Group, an informa business

© 2019 Taylor & Francis

The right of Tara Goldstein to be identified as author of this work has been asserted by her in accordance with sections 77 and 78 of the Copyright, Designs and Patents Act 1988.

Library of Congress Cataloging-in-Publication Data
A catalog record for this title has been requested

ISBN: 978-1-138-38713-3 (hbk)
ISBN: 978-1-138-38714-0 (pbk)
ISBN: 978-0-429-42642-1 (ebk)

Typeset in Adobe Caslon
by Integra Software Services Pvt. Ltd.

Dedication

To the parents, children, youth, and educators who have participated in the LGBTQ Families Speak Out project (2014–2020) at the Ontario Institute for Studies in Education, University of Toronto. Thank you.

Contents

Acknowledgements

First, I'd like to acknowledge and thank all the students and colleagues who have worked on sexuality, gender, and schooling research projects with me over the last 16 years and the students and colleagues who have taught and contributed to the development of the OISE course on sexuality, gender, and schooling. They are Pam Baer, Nina Bascia, Kathy Bickmore, Alec Butler, Sarah Sookie Bardwell, Anthony Collins, Katerina Cook, Edil Ga'al, Michael Halder, benjamin lee hicks, Tarra Joshi, Austen Koecher, June Larkin, Yasmin Owis, Bob Phillips, Kate Reid, Vanessa Russell, Jenny Salisbury, Susan Sturman, Heather Sykes, Jeffrey White, and Jocelyn Wickett. The letters that appear in this book are the result of the many, many rich and challenging conversations we've had together.

I would also like to acknowledge all of the wonderful guest speakers who have visited my classes over the years to share their expertise and skills. You are too many to name, but you know who you are! Many thanks.

I have several colleagues and friends from Australia who have also engaged in many conversations about sexuality, gender, and schooling with me. They are Judith Chapman, Heather Cobban, Cristyn Davies, Catherine Doherty, Tania Ferfolja, Susan Grieshaber, Cushla Kapitzke, Jo Lampert, Allan Luke, Carmen Luke, Kerry Robinson, and Jacqueline Ullman. Thank you for our talks and for your friendship.

Both my research and teaching on sexuality, gender, and schooling have been made possible by several vital institutions and programs: the Social Sciences and Humanities Research Council of Canada (SSHRCC); the Department of Curriculum, Teaching and Learning at the Ontario Institute of Studies in Education (OISE), University of Toronto; the Office of the Associate Dean, Research, International & Innovation at OISE; the University of Toronto Research Services; the University of Toronto Award of Excellence program for undergraduate students; and the University of Toronto Work-Study program. Over the years, dozens of people from the University of Toronto have supported my research and teaching, but there are two people who I want to acknowledge and thank here: Bessie Giannikos, Manager, Finance and Administration; and Cheryl Clarke, Program Assistant, Graduate Studies in the Department of Curriculum, Teaching and Learning. Without Bessie and Cheryl's work to help me design budgets for my projects and pay research assistants and guest artists who have worked with me, much of the work that has informed this book would not have taken place.

One of the graduate students I'm currently working with, benjamin lee hicks, wrote "The Unicorn Glossary" which appears at the end of the book. I want to thank benjamin for the time they spent updating the glossary so I could include it in this book. Two other graduate students I am working with, Jenny Salisbury and Pam Baer, co-wrote the script *Out at School* with me and I want to thank them for their deep commitment to the project.

Finally, I'd like to acknowledge and thank Kate Reid (again) for her excellent editing of the final draft of the book and the editors and staff at Taylor & Francis who brought the book into publication: Naomi Silverman, Catherine Bernard, Rachel Dugan, and copy editor Roger Browning. This book has come into the world because of your hard work. Many thanks to you all.

INTRODUCTION: LETTER 1

GETTING ACQUAINTED

Dear Teacher:

This book contains a series of letters I've written about how to expect, welcome, and support lesbian, gay, bisexual, transgender, and queer (LGBTQ) students and families in school. I use the initialism LGBTQ (lesbian, gay, bisexual, trans, and queer) to include people who identify as transgender, transsexual, Two-Spirit, questioning, intersex, asexual, pansexual, ally, agender, gender queer, gender variant, and/or pangender. If some of these words are unfamiliar to you, don't worry. You will find an explanation of some of them in the letters that follow and a definition of all of them at the end of this book in "The Unicorn Glossary," written by benjamin lee hicks.[1]

While I have just named some of the different ways people currently identify under the initials LGBTQ, I've learned that the ways people describe their gender and sexual identities are always evolving. This means the list I've put together for this book will change over time. I've also learned that, when I talk about people's identities, I show respect by using the names and pronouns people use themselves. If I'm not sure how people identify, I've learned to ask.

In writing these letters, I have drawn upon the discussions I've had with students enrolled in a teacher education course on sexuality, gender, and schooling that has been taught at the Ontario Institute of Studies in Education (OISE) at the University of Toronto for 16 years.[2] The course began in 2001 as a discussion group for teacher education students who identified as LGBTQ. The group talked about ways of dealing with homophobic slurs and name-calling at school, whether or not to come out as LGBTQ to colleagues and students, and how to include LGBTQ content into their classroom curriculum. The discussion group was our teacher education program's Gay Straight Alliance (GSA) (if you're not sure what a GSA is, see Letter 2).

After the group had successfully run for a year, my colleague Bob Phillips and I decided to turn the discussion group into an elective course, moving our sexuality education work from the margins of OISE's teacher education programming to its centre. In January 2003 the course became the first and only 36-hour teacher education course in Canada to feature conversations about sexuality at school. When the course was first offered it focused on discussions of homophobia, heterosexism, and heteronormativity. More recently, it has also taken up discussions of gender expression, gender transition, and the socio-political factors that affect transgender and gender diverse students and families.

Moving from a short history of OISE's course on sexuality, gender, and schooling to a description of the letters I've written, you'll see that the book has been divided into three parts. Part 1 includes a set of letters about teaching sexuality at school; Part 2 contains a set of letters about gender at school; and Part 3 comprises letters about the experiences of LGBTQ families in school.[3] But, before you read any further, I'd like to tell you a little about my past and current research, which has informed my thinking around teaching about gender and sexuality at school.

My First Research Study on Anti-Homophobia Education at School

My first research study on anti-homophobia education at school began in 2001. I wanted to find out how, if at all, principals and teachers working in four different schools at the Toronto District School Board (TDSB) had been able to implement their new anti-homophobia equity policy.[4] I also wanted to find out in what ways, if any, had implementing the policy created tensions and conflicts for principals and teachers. The 18-month study ran from 2001–2003 and included one elementary school, one middle school, and two high schools. I worked with a research team of three students: doctoral student Susan Sturman, and undergraduate students Anthony Collins and Michael

Halder. As a team we identified as cisgender and either lesbian or gay. Three of us identified as White and one of us as Pakistani. I identify as cisgender, lesbian, and White

Using an analytic framework called the Triangle Model[5] we found that teachers and principals who were trying to challenge homophobia in their schools needed to address homophobic *ideas* that circulated about LGBTQ people.

They also needed to address *individual actions and practices* of homophobia, such as name-calling and homophobic bullying. Finally, they needed to address *institutional forms* of homophobia; for example, school curriculum that completely excluded LGBTQ people. We also found that teachers and principals who had begun implementing anti-homophobia education were afraid that their school's commitments to LGBTQ rights might collide with some of their parents' religious beliefs about homosexuality, a topic I take up in Letters 4 and 5.[6]

When the study was completed I wanted to find a compelling way to share the findings with principals, teachers, students, and parents. So, I wrote a play script called *Snakes and Ladders* based on the major findings of the study that could be read aloud and discussed by teachers and principals in a class or at a conference. While the characters in the play are fictional, the conflicts featured in the play actually took place and were documented in the research.

Snakes and Ladders tells the story of what happens when a group of high-school teachers and students attempts to put on Pride Week at their school. Coalitions are built, homophobia is resisted and reproduced, and teachers and students learn that they can't take their human rights for granted. Originally written in 2004, and updated and edited in 2010 for publication in the International Journal of Curriculum and Pedagogy,[7] the

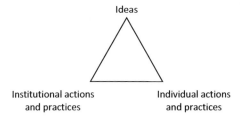

The Triangle Model

play is included at the end of this book, after "The Unicorn Glossary." Several of the letters in Part 1, entitled Sexuality at School, discuss the findings of the research as they have been represented in particular scenes in *Snakes and Ladders*. After reading these letters you may be interested in reading and discussing the entire script with your colleagues and students. A list of discussion questions is included at the end of the play.

My Current Research on Gender and Sexuality at School

While my first research project focused on the anti-homophobia education work of four schools in the city of Toronto, my current research study involves interviewing between 35 and 40 LGBTQ families across the province of Ontario about their experiences at school. I'm also interested in how families work with teachers and principals to create safer and more supportive learning environments for their children. The six-year study, which we named *LGBTQ Families Speak Out*, began in 2014 and will end in 2020. I have worked on the study with five doctoral, one Master and four undergraduate students: Pam Baer, Austen Koecher, benjamin lee hicks, Jenny Salisbury, Kate Reid, Tarra Joshi, Katrina Cook, Alec Butler, Edil Ga'al, and Yasmin Owis. They each self-identify in the following ways: Pam Baer identifies as agender, queer, and White; Austen Koecher identifies as cisgender, White, and a child of a queer family; benjamin lee hicks identifies as genderqueer/trans, pansexual, and White; Jenny Salisbury identifies as a cis, straight, White woman of Dutch and Canadian settler heritage; Kate Reid identifies as queer and White; Tarra Joshi identifies as cisgender, South Asian/White; Katrina Cook identifies as a White woman and a child of a queer family; Alec Butler identifies as non-binary, intersex, Two-Spirit, Indigenous/settler; Edil Ga'al identifies as a Black woman; and Yasmin Owis identifies as a queer/bisexual, cisgender woman of colour. In Part 2, Gender at School, and Part 3, LGBTQ Families at School, I include excerpts from a number of the interviews and use the insights of the families to talk about a variety of experiences. In addition to reading what several of the families have to say, you can also view video clips from their interviews on our website: www.lgbtqfamiliesspeakout.ca.

Some of the names of the interviewees in this book are pseudonyms while others are not. Our team's practice concerning the use of pseudonyms is to provide our participants with the opportunity to use a pseudonym when excerpts of their interviews are uploaded on to our website. Additionally they are able to choose to be anonymous by having their faces blurred and their voices changed. Our interview participants also have an opportunity to review their edited video interview excerpts before we upload them onto our website, and/or tell us if there is an excerpt that they would rather not appear on the website. If there is an excerpt they don't want on the website, we don't upload it. As well, if any of our participants change their mind about having their interview being available online, we remove it from the website.

However, when it comes to publishing the results of our research we encourage all our research participants to choose a pseudonym, because once someone's name has been published alongside their words that person can never be made anonymous. For this reason many participants have taken up our suggestion to choose a pseudonym. In this book, I indicate someone's name is a pseudonym by putting the word "pseudonym" in parentheses beside their name; for example, Violet Addley (pseudonym). Others have asked us to use their real names because they are engaged in LGBTQ advocacy and activism and feel their lives and identities are already public. Therefore, they want our writing about their experiences at school to be attributed to them without a pseudonym. Finally, we have interviewed several children in this project. When we publish findings associated with any of the children's interviews, we only use pseudonyms.

Recently the research team has written a series of verbatim theatre scripts about the experiences of LGBTQ families in Ontario schools. The series is called *Out at School*. Unlike *Snakes and Ladders*, which features fictional characters who are involved in conflicts that were documented in my first sexuality and schooling research study, each script in the *Out at School* series is made up of a set of monologues that have been solely created from our interviewees' own words. When we perform one of the scripts, the monologues are accompanied by a set of visual images created by team member benjamin lee hicks and original songs composed by team member Kate Reid. *Out at School* is a work in progress and will develop over the next few years. Our most current performance script appears with a list of discussion questions at the end of this book after *Snakes and Ladders*. The team follows the same practice of using pseudonyms in *Out at School* that we do in our other writing.

As you read through the letters in this book, you may experience a moment or two that unsettles you. Or you may experience a moment that pushes you to ask questions about what you know and what you don't know. Some of the letters may provoke you to reassess a cherished teaching practice or belief. While working through unsettling questions can be uncomfortable, my students tell me that learning to ask questions about their beliefs and teaching practices has helped them become more accountable to LGBTQ students, parents, and colleagues. It helps them become the best teachers they can be. I hope this is your experience, too.

All the best,
Tara Goldstein
Toronto, July 2018

Notes

1 benjamin lee hicks has made an intentional choice not to capitalize their name.

2 Over the last 16 years, my colleagues Vanessa Russell, who is currently working as a teacher at the Toronto District School Board, and Heather Sykes, who teaches with me at OISE, have also taught the course. In the last several years OISE PhD students Pam Baer, Austen Koecher, and benjamin lee hicks have co-taught the course with me. The pedagogical ideas I discuss in these letters have been developed over the years in collaboration with Vanessa, Heather, Pam, Austen, and benjamin.

3 The book is called *Teaching Gender and Sexuality at School* because this is the way the field of gender and sexuality education has come to name itself (the word gender appears before the word sexuality). I begin with letters about teaching sexuality because that's the way I began my own work. I started by teaching and researching the ways homophobia, heterosexism, and heteronormativity had an impact on people's lives in school. More recently, I have engaged with the experiences of transgender and gender diverse children and youth at school.

4 The Toronto District School Board's equity policy was approved in 1999 and published in 2000. However, many of the schools in the TDSB had been involved in equity education before the policy was approved. In January 1998 the Ontario government legislated forced amalgamation of the former Toronto Board of Education with five other Metro Toronto

boards to create the TDSB. Each of these six school boards had its own equity policies, and work was needed to amalgamate them. The equity policy published in 2000 represents this amalgamation work. In 2000, the policy contained six sections. The first section presented the board's Equity Foundation Statement. The other five sections presented the board's five parallel commitments to equity policy implementation. There were commitments to (1) anti-racism and ethnocultural equity; (2) anti-sexism and gender equity; (3) anti-homophobia, sexual orientation and equity; (4) anti-classism and socio-economic equity; and (5) equity for persons with disabilities. The five parallel commitment documents are no longer available on the TDSB's website. However, a copy of the current Equity Foundation Statement, Human Rights Policy and Procedures is available at: http://www.tdsb.on.ca/HighSchool/Equityinclu sion/Guidelinespolicies.aspx.

5 For further discussion about the Triangle Model, see McCaskell, 2005.

6 For further discussion of the findings see Goldstein, Collins, and Halder, 2007.

7 See Goldstein, 2010.

PART 1
SEXUALITY AT SCHOOL

LETTER 2
GAY STRAIGHT ALLIANCES

Dear Teacher:

I want to begin this section on sexuality at school by introducing you to a teacher named Rachel Davis, who is a character in my ethnographic play script *Snakes and Ladders,* included at the end of this book. Rachel and the other characters in the play are fictional composites of the real-life teachers, principals, and students the research team interviewed. Rachel runs her school's Gay Straight Alliance (GSA) and identifies as lesbian, cisgender, and White. As you may know, GSAs are student clubs created by teachers and/or students to create safer and more welcoming schools for LGBTQ students and families. Most GSAs include one or two teachers who serve as faculty advisors. In the last few years, many schools have renamed their GSAs to be more accurate and inclusive of the diverse ways their members identify and to open up conversations about gender. For example, some GSAs call themselves the Gender and Sexual Orientation Alliance, the Queer Straight Alliance, the Rainbow Alliance, the Pride Club, the Ally Club, and the Diversity Club.

GSAs are important. Recent research shows Canadian students who go to a school with a GSA are more likely to report their schools are supportive of LGBTQ people. They are also much more likely to be open or "out" with their peers about their sexual and/or gender identity, and are more likely to say their school climate is becoming less homophobic.[1] Similarly, research undertaken in the United States demonstrates that schools with a GSA report lower levels of anti-LGBTQ harassment and bullying.[2]

As I explained in my Getting Acquainted letter, *Snakes and Ladders* is based on research findings from an 18-month study I conducted from 2001–2003. The study examined a variety of anti-homophobia education initiatives in four different public schools run by the Toronto District School Board: one elementary, one middle school, and two high schools. At the time, the board was responsible for the operation of 555 elementary and secondary public schools in the city of Toronto. The board was not only the largest school board in Canada, it was (and still is) among the most ethnoculturally diverse in the world. Among the most important findings of the study were the personal tensions and conflicts many teachers experienced when they tried to undertake anti-homophobia education in their diverse schools.[3] *Snakes and Ladders* examines these tensions and conflicts.

The play begins when Rachel tells her new principal that her GSA group wants to put on a Pride Day. Like Pride parades that take place all over the world annually, the school's Pride Day would celebrate LGBTQ lives and culture. The principal is named Karen Diamond and she identifies as straight, cisgender, and White.

Karen, who didn't know there was a GSA at the school, raises concerns about the group. In scene 1, she tells Rachel, "Most parents don't want their children to hear about regular sex at school, never mind gay sex." Rachel tries to explain that the group doesn't spend time talking about sex, they talk about homophobia, but Karen cuts her off. After the meeting, Rachel shares her frustration with her colleague Anne James, the faculty advisor of the school's anti-racism group STAR (Students and Teachers Against Racism). Anne identifies as straight, cisgender, and Black. In scene 3, Rachel tells Anne, "I tried to explain that it wasn't a gay group and that we were talking about homophobia, not sex. But she couldn't hear me. For her, talking about gay issues means talking about sex. Homosexuals are homo-*sex*-uals."

Anne is sympathetic and comes up with a plan. She suggests the GSA and STAR work together to organize a set of Pride Days during the school's Anti-Racism Week: Racial Pride, Ethnic Pride, and Gay Pride. While some school principals won't support an initiative that specifically focuses on homophobia, they will support an event that focuses on social justice or human rights more generally. Anne thinks Karen might approve a set of Pride Days that are undertaken during Anti-Racism Week.

The teachers we interviewed in our study told us that finding school allies when there is concern or opposition to an anti-homophobia education proposal is an excellent strategy for moving forward in the face of opposition or resistance, and in the play Karen eventually approves Anti-Racism and Pride Week after she consults with a more experienced principal working in her school board. However, creating alliances across student groups and experiences of oppression can be challenging. When Anne pitches her idea to the students in STAR they aren't as open to the idea as she had hoped.

RAY (STAR STUDENT): Why do we have to have Gay Pride Day during Anti-Racism Week?

DIANE (STAR STUDENT): Yeah. Why don't they celebrate it sometime in June when other gay people celebrate it? March 21 is supposed to be about racism.

ROBERTO (STUDENT TEACHER): Some people experience racism *and* homophobia. We need to fight both together.

DIANE: Black people aren't faggots.

HELEN (GSA STUDENT): *(Angry)* What?

RACHEL: *(Calm)* Okay. Hold it there. *(To DIANE)* The last word you used. What was it?

DIANE: *(Embarrassed)* What? Faggots?

RACHEL: Right. How is faggot used in the hallway? Is it a compliment?

HELEN: No.

DIANE: It's not a put down.

RACHEL: Although some people might use it as a joke, I think the consensus is that it's usually used as a put down. So we won't use it. Okay?

DIANE: : Okay.

RACHEL: Okay. Before we continue with the proposal, let's talk about the idea that Black people aren't lesbian and gay. Is that true?

RAY: On television, the only people who are gay are White.

HELEN: Gay people aren't only White. My brother is Chinese and he's gay. He went to this school last year but had to leave because he was harassed for being a "faggot" . . .

. . . DIANE: If we help out with Gay Day, people might think that we're gay.

HELEN: I'm going to help out and I'm not gay.

DIANE: But some people may think you are.

CHRIS (GSA STUDENT): What's wrong with people thinking that you're gay?

(DIANE is silent. There's an awkward pause.)

ANNE: Mr. Rodriguez, why don't you tell us the ideas you and Ms. Davis have come up with for Gay Pride Day.

CHRIS: We should call it LGBTQ Pride Day.

ANNE: Let's hear from Mr. Rodriguez first. We'll talk about the name after.

ROBERTO: Okay. We talked about inviting a group called T.E.A.C.H. to come and do an anti-homophobia workshop with us. T.E.A.C.H. stands for Teens Educating and Confronting Homophobia. The members of T.E.A.C.H. identify as LGBTQ and straight.

HELEN: Are they all White?

ROBERTO: No. The group is mixed. And, as part of the workshop, they tell their coming-out stories. The story of when they first knew they might not be or weren't heterosexual. We also thought about holding a special game of Snakes and Ladders on Canadian minority history.

CHRIS: What about a queer talent night? And a drag contest?

DIANE: What's drag?

HELEN: It's when guys dress up like girls and girls dress up like guys.

CHRIS: Or maybe we could put on an "Ask Dr. Ruth" show with questions and answers about queer sex.

The students' discussion is interrupted by the appearance of the principal, Karen Diamond, who, despite having approved Anti-Racism and Pride Week, has her own issues with the students' discussion and their emerging plans.

KAREN: Ms. James and the STAR group have a lot of experience conducting anti-racist education and I am sure that this experience will be helpful to the GSA. But I am concerned about some of the ideas I have heard you talk about. I read the board's pamphlet on "What Anti-Homophobia Education Is and What It Isn't." *(To student CHRIS)* The board is clear that anti-homophobia education is *not* sex education. So, there will be no question and answer show about sex.

CHRIS: But . . .

KAREN: Which brings me to another concern, which is about language. Lots of people don't like that word you used.

CHRIS: Which word?

KAREN: Queer. It makes them uncomfortable. So, I suggest, insist really, you not use it. Since there is some confusion about the term LG – B – QT – GLTB – you know what I mean – and the term transgender, I also suggest you stick with the name Gay Pride Day.

CHRIS: But not all queers are gay. Some are bi, some are . . .

KAREN: People will understand that you are using the word "gay" to mean all people who are not heterosexual. Finally, (*looks directly at student teacher RAHIMA*) given the religious diversity present in this school, we need to be careful not to offend anyone. This is a school, not a nightclub. So, no gay talent night and no drag contest. The T.E.A.C. H. workshop is approved by the board so it's fine. You can contact someone at the board's Equity Office for a list of other resources. (*Looks at her watch, stands up to leave*) I'm sorry, but I have to go. Good luck in your planning. Keep me informed of your progress. I want to see the final program for the entire week.

When my teacher education students and I discuss these scenes from *Snakes and Ladders* we talk about how high school students bring different understandings and knowledge about homophobia and LGBTQ lives to school. While some high school students like Chris are leading openly gay lives and have a wealth of knowledge about homophobia and anti-homophobia education, others like Ray and Diane are discussing homo-phobia for the first time. We then talk about the importance of providing students with definitions of terms and language commonly used in gender and sexuality education work (for definitions of these terms, see "The Unicorn Glossary" at the end of this book). We also talk about the importance of challenging the use of any derogatory words about LGBTQ people, whether they are used intentionally or not.

Both new and experienced teachers often find it difficult to find the words they need to challenge homophobic name-calling and they appreciate the model provided by Rachel. Rachel's response to the use of "faggot" in the Anti-Racism and Pride Week discussion was modelled after a teacher response filmed in Debra Chasnoff and Helen Cohen's documentary film, *It's Elementary: Talking About Gay Issues in School.*[4] *It's Elementary* is an excellent pedagogical tool for anti-homophobia teacher education, and all of the Pride Week activities mentioned in the play are demonstrated in the film. A brief description of the film is included in the "Resources" section of this book.

Another discussion that often takes place in my class concerns the difficulty of addressing racism and homophobia simultaneously. When Anne and Rachel suggest forming an alliance to challenge both forms of discrimination during Anti-Racism and Pride Week, Diane worries that working on homophobia will shift the focus away from work on anti-racism. Competition for time and resources is one of the barriers that can hinder, if not undermine, the success of an alliance between anti-racism and anti-homophobia educators. To challenge the divisiveness of "we and them," student teacher Roberto, who identifies as gay and Brown, responds by saying "Some people experience racism *and* homophobia. We need to fight both together." Roberto's response, which refers to the way that LGBTQ people of colour experience intersecting or multiple forms of oppression, provides my students and me with a productive theoretical and political framework for pursuing our discussion of the possibilities and challenges of coalition building in anti-oppression education work.[5]

American legal scholar Kimberlé Crenshaw first coined the term "intersectionality" almost 30 years ago in 1989.[6] In a TED Talk she gave in 2016, Crenshaw explained: "Many years ago I began to use the term intersectionality to deal with the fact that many of our social justice problems, like racism and sexism, are often overlapping, creating multiple levels of social injustice."[7] To illustrate how racism and sexism overlap, Crenshaw described the situation of an African-American woman named Emma DeGraffenreid who claimed she was not hired for a job at a local car manufacturing plant because she was a Black woman. She brought her claim to court but the judge dismissed her suit. He argued that the employer did hire African-Americans and did hire women. What the judge was not willing to acknowledge, however, was that the African-Americans, who were hired for industrial and maintenance work, were men. The women the employer hired for secretarial or front-office work were White.

As a student of anti-discriminatory law, Crenshaw was struck by DeGraffenreid's case. It felt like "injustice squared." She realized there was no name for DeGraffenreid's dilemma, and when there's no name for a problem it is hard to see it and think about ways to solve it. Crenshaw came up with a way to name DeGraffenreid's problem by using the analogy of the intersection of a road. She describes the dilemma like this. There were two roads to the intersection where DeGraffenreid stood. One road represented race and the other road represented gender. The traffic on those roads were the hiring policies at the car manufacturing plant. The race road had policies that encouraged the hiring of African-American men. The gender road had policies that encouraged the hiring of White women. But because DeGraffenreid was both Black and female, she was positioned precisely where those roads overlapped and was excluded from both the company's race and gender hiring practices. DeGraffenreid wasn't an African-American man so she couldn't be hired for industrial or maintenance work. She wasn't a White woman, so she couldn't be hired for secretarial or office work. She was caught in the intersection. After naming DeGraffenreid's problem, Crenshaw went on to write about discrimination at other intersections; for example, discrimination at the intersections of race and heterosexism, transphobia, xenophobia, and ableism.

When thinking about how to apply the concept of intersectionality to the practice of teaching, my students and I talk about the different ways LGBTQ students and families experience discrimination at a variety of intersections. For example, as parent Victoria Mason told us in her interview for the LGBTQ Families Speak Out research project (see Letter 17), one of the reasons her daughter asked her not to come out as a lesbian at school had to do with the fact that she was the only student of colour in her class. Victoria's daughter was already racially marked at school and had to deal with being marginalized because of her race. She didn't want to also be marginalized because she was a child with a lesbian mother. After analyzing the ways some LGBTQ families and students experience intersectional discrimination, we talk about what teachers can do to support them.

To begin thinking about the ways you might support students and families who face discrimination at an intersection, you may find the ideas listed on the GLSEN website helpful (www.glsen.org). GLSEN (Gay, Lesbian, Straight Education Network) is an American organization that works to create safer and more affirming schools for LGBTQ students. In a blog about being a good ally, GLSEN provides a list of actions teachers can take to support LGBTQ students with intersectional identities. For example, teachers can read GLSEN's report *Shared Differences: The Experiences of LGBT Students of Color in Our Nation's Schools*.[8] Teachers can also make sure their GSAs celebrate the impact of the achievements of people of colour during Asian and Pacific Islander Heritage Month, Black History Month,

Latinx Heritage Month, and Native American Heritage Month. In Canada, the names of some of these celebrations are a little different. For example, in Ontario, we celebrate Asian and South Asian Heritage Month, Hispanic Latin American Heritage Month, and National Indigenous History Month. Finally, GSAs can also form alliances with anti-racist student groups and work on issues of racism, homophobia, and gender exclusion together, like the GSA and STAR in *Snakes and Ladders*. While events such as Black History Month and Pride Week in *Snakes and Ladders* are important for recognizing, celebrating, and educating about particular communities, I understand they are only able to provide isolated and short-term access to voice and visibility. I also understand that these events do little to challenge the privilege of those in power in schools.

Returning briefly to *Snakes and Ladders*, despite the tensions involved in pursuing both anti-racist and anti-homophobia initiatives, at the end of the play, Pride Week takes place at the school. The students from both STAR and the GSA learn a lot about challenging homophobia and racism together, and so do the students who aren't members of the clubs but who participate in Pride Week.

If your school doesn't have a GSA yet, and you'd like to start one, GLSEN offers information on how to create a GSA, find members, and run an effective meeting. Beginning or participating in a GSA at your school is a great place to start gender and sexuality education work.

All the best,
Tara

Notes

1 See Taylor and Peter with McMinn, Elliott, Beldom, Ferry, Gross, Paquin, and Schachter, 2011.
2 See Kosciw, Greytak, Giga, Villenas, and Danischewski, 2015. The results of the 2017 survey will be released in the fall of 2018 on the GLSEN website: https://www.glsen.org.
3 See Goldstein, Collins, and Halder, 2007.
4 See Chasnoff and Cohen, 1996.
5 For an excellent resource on the intersections between race and queer sexuality, see Kumashiro, 2001.
6 See Crenshaw, 1989.
7 See Crenshaw, 2016.
8 See Diaz and Kosciw, 2009.

LETTER 3
WHAT WILL THE PARENTS SAY?

Dear Teacher:

One of the fears teachers have when they begin thinking about doing anti-homophobia education work is the fear of parent opposition. In the interviews we did in the 2001–2003 research project on anti-homophobia education practices at school, teachers told us they were worried that parents would think their children shouldn't learn about LGBTQ people at school.[1] When I asked the coordinator of the Toronto District School Board's Human Sexuality Program how to address teachers' concerns about the possibility of being reprimanded for their anti-homophobia education work, he suggested they start an ongoing dialogue with their parent community about all the topics they will be discussing over the school year. This piece of advice was also given by one of the high-school principals I interviewed: "Make sure everybody's on board; your trustees, your superintendent, your parents ..."[2] It's important to highlight here the Human Sexuality Coordinator's use of the words "all topics" in his advice to teachers. When teachers begin conversations with parents, it shouldn't only be about the gender and sexuality work they are doing in their classroom; it should be about *all* of their classroom work. When activities about gender and sexuality are the only activities parents are consulted on, they are framed as controversial rather than inclusive of diversity.

Like the teachers in my research study, Karen Diamond, the principal in the play *Snakes and Ladders,* also worries about what parents think. At the beginning of the play, she rejects the GSA's proposal to organize a Pride Week because she thinks the parents at her school will object. However, after she consults with her mentor, Bob Byers, she learns that events like Anti-Racism and Pride Week are important because they work towards creating a safer and more supportive school environment for LGBTQ students and families. She also learns that her school board has an anti-homophobia equity policy (as well as an anti-racism policy) which she is expected to implement.

Bob identifies as straight, cisgender, and White. When he talks to Karen about her fear that parents won't support Pride Week, he shares a personal story with her. In scene 8, he tells her his daughter is a lesbian who came out in her first year of university. He also reveals that, when his daughter came out, he went into the closet:

BOB: I was scared to tell anyone. Even close friends. I was afraid of what they might say to me. I was also afraid for her safety. Would she get harassed? Would people call her ugly names? But I couldn't talk about it. I couldn't reach out. A few weeks later I was asked to go to a professional development session on the board's new equity policy. When they talked about the five new equity implementation documents and told us that one of them was about challenging homophobia, I felt grateful. Really grateful. I wanted every school, every university to have a document like that so that my daughter and kids like her would be safe. After the session I talked to one of the equity people about Shannon. That was the first time I came out about having a daughter who is lesbian.

KAREN: Wow.

BOB: But in order for the policy to do any good, we have to implement it. Even when it's difficult. Even when it brings us into conflict with staff and parents. Karen, the policy needs to be implemented. I'll support you.

Karen is surprised by Bob's story. She's never met anyone who had a child who identified as LGBTQ, and has never thought about what kinds of concerns they might have. When Bob tells her ". . . in order for the policy to do any good, we have to implement it. Even when it's difficult. Even when it brings us into conflict with staff and parents," Karen understands the urgency behind his request. She also understands, perhaps for the first time, that for some parents the education

Anti-Racism and Pride Week provides is critical to their children's safety and well-being.

However, Karen doesn't consult with the school's parent community before or after approving Anti-Racism and Pride Week. As a result she finds herself having a dialogue with parents at one of her school council meetings. A parent has heard about Anti-Racism and Pride Week and has called his school superintendent with concerns about the event. The superintendent suggests the parent attend the next school council meeting and raise his questions there. While there was only one parent complaint to the superintendent, three parents, who identify as straight and cisgender, participate in the school council discussion in scene 14, the last scene of the play.

Karen begins the meeting by making sure everyone knows that all of the activities planned for Anti-Racism and Pride Week are an attempt to implement the board's equity policy. Even though several parents at the meeting may not support the school's plans, as a principal who works at the board she knows she is expected to implement the equity policy. It's part of her job to create a safer, more supportive, and more inclusive school environment for LGBTQ students and families.

KAREN: *(Looks at her watch)* Good evening everyone. It's now 8 o'clock. Let's begin. There are several items on tonight's agenda. We're going to begin with a discussion on Anti-Racism and Pride Week so that those of you who are here for this particular discussion can leave as soon as it's done. *(Takes a deep breath)* Two of our faculty, Rachel Davis and Anne James, have prepared a list of the activities taking place this week at Pierre Elliot Trudeau. That list is being circulated. Ms. Davis has also copied the board's Equity Foundation Statement for you to read. All of our activities this week are an attempt to implement the board's equity policy. *(Pauses)* The floor is open for questions and comments.

PARENT 1: I am a parent with two kids in this school. I don't want my kids learning about homosexuality from gay and lesbian guest speakers who have been invited to the school to share their coming-out stories. Our church teaches that homosexuality is wrong. We do not believe it's a normal lifestyle. It is not the school's place to contradict what we teach our children at home.

PARENT 2: Even if you don't believe in the gay lifestyle, and you feel that this is against your religion and not a good thing and against God, don't you think it's helpful that the school opens the topic so that you can teach what you believe to your child? It's hard to talk about this. So when our kids come home with questions, it opens the dialogue. Even if you are against *(makes imaginary quotation marks with her hands)* "the lifestyle," don't you think it still needs to be addressed?

PARENT 1: Not by the school.

ANNE: My church also taught me that to be gay or lesbian was wrong. And I brought that with me because I don't stop being Christian when I walk into the building. So I have had to work really hard coming to terms with what I've been taught. Because I know that in my classroom, at my school, I have to be there for all my students. I have to affirm who they are and that includes kids of gay and lesbian families and kids who may be gay or lesbian themselves. I know what it's like not to be affirmed at school. I want my students' school experience to be different.

PARENT 3: I agree that we shouldn't throw stones. But I don't believe that we should be using taxpayers' money for promoting homosexuality either. It's up to parents to teach their children about sexuality, according to their own set of moral values.

PARENT 1: I agree.

RACHEL: It's not appropriate that values only be taught at home. There are social values, community values. When teachers allow one student to hurl the word "faggot" at another and don't address the issue, I think it's unconscionable. What message does the student get? The student gets the message that it's okay to verbally assault gay people. If it weren't, then the teacher would step in. And what happens when the student who was called a "faggot" suspects they're gay and needs to talk to someone about it? He thinks "I can't let anyone know. They'll think there's something wrong with me. Because when I was called a 'faggot' last year they thought it was okay."

HELEN: My brother Jeffrey used to be a student at this school. And when he was in Grade 9 he was called a "faggot" almost every day. When he finally told me what was going on I tried to help him. But there wasn't anything that I could do on my own. Jeffrey finally got so depressed that he refused to go to school. That's when my parents decided to transfer him to another school.

RAHIMA (STUDENT TEACHER): What Helen has just said is very important. We need to stop the name-calling that goes on in our school. Many of the events that have been planned for Anti-Racism and Pride Week have been designed to help us do that.

CHRIS: Homophobia is not only about name-calling. It's also about being beat up.

ROBERTO: In addition to the issue of gay bashing, there's the issue of suicide. The amount of suicides and attempted suicides by gay, lesbian, and questioning youth is alarming. Thirty percent of all youth suicides are undertaken by gay and lesbian youth.[3] Because our society is saying it's not okay to be gay, kids think that they aren't okay. So what do they do? They try to kill themselves. We are not taking good care of our kids.

SARA (STUDENT TEACHER): When I was growing up, nobody ever gave me any sense that it was okay to be who I was, a lesbian, or that there was support, resources for me, anything. I want to help the students I teach to grow up knowing, grow up feeling it's okay and not to feel so isolated. At some churches they believe that there is God in every person and those people include queer people too.

PARENT 1: That's fine for people who attend those churches, but not for me. All I am asking is that the school respect my religious beliefs by not bringing any discussion of homosexuality into my children's classroom.

RACHEL: If you want the school to respect your religious beliefs, then you need to respect the stance we take about teaching about tolerance for others.

(All three student teachers and the students from the GSA and STAR applaud. Some of the students whistle.)

(To ANNE) I can't believe I said tolerance.

ANNE: Whatever gets the job done.

CHRIS: As a school, I think we have to do more than teach about tolerance. I don't want to be tolerated. I want to be respected for who I am. A gay teenager.

PARENT 2: We live in a world where the person in the next cubicle to you at work could be gay. You don't have to believe in what they do or what they think or say, but you do have to be able to work with them.

(There is a pause in the discussion.)

KAREN: *(Looks at her watch)* Well, it's getting late. Can we move on to other business? Or are there other comments or questions?

PARENT 1: I have a comment. I call on you, as principal of this school, to prohibit any further discussion of homosexuality during the school day.

PARENT 3: Or at least require permission slips for students to attend the sessions on homosexuality.

RACHEL: *(Angry)* If you want us to send home permission slips to talk about gay and lesbian lives, do you want us to also send home slips to talk about African-Canadian lives or Chinese lives or women's lives? I really have a problem with that, I really do.

ANNE: Your point's well taken. At the same time, as the members of STAR, Students and Teachers Against Racism, will tell you, we still have a long way to go before we can say the school curriculum does a good job of affirming all our students' lives.

KAREN: Well, there's been a lot of food for thought shared here tonight. I want to think carefully about what everyone has said tonight. I also want to undertake an in-depth assessment of what students have learned from this year's Anti-Racism and Pride Week before making any decisions about its future. I'll report the results of the assessment at our next school council meeting.

PARENT 1: Well, you can be sure my kids won't be attending any of the gay activities.

KAREN: Thank you all for your participation in this discussion. We're going to move on, now, to the next item of business, the government's community service requirement.

After Parent 1 asks her to prohibit any further discussion of homosexuality during the school day, and Parent 3 suggests she send permission slips home to talk about LGBTQ people, Karen ends the discussion by telling everyone she will undertake an assessment of Anti-Racism and Pride Week and report on the results at the next school council meeting. She knows the equity policy prevents her from prohibiting the discussion of homosexuality at school and she knows she isn't required to ask parents for permission to talk about LGBTQ lives at school. However, instead of directly responding to Parent 1 and Parent 3, she presents Anti-Racism and Pride Week as a pilot project that she will evaluate and report back on. This strategy frames Anti-Racism and Pride Week as an important learning activity for students, an activity that is going to be evaluated just like other school activities. Anti-Racism and Pride Week has been granted the institutional support it needs.

Before ending this letter, I want to discuss Rachel's use of the word "tolerance" during the school council meeting. I also want to talk about which parent voices are missing from scene 14 of *Snakes and Ladders.* Rachel uses the word "tolerance" in response to a parent who asks Karen to respect his religious beliefs. Rachel tells the parent, "If you want the school to respect your religious beliefs then you need to respect the stance we take about teaching about tolerance for others." As soon as the words are out of her mouth, Rachel tells her friend and colleague Anne, "I can't believe I said 'tolerance'." Rachel's student Chris is also unhappy with Rachel's use of the word tolerance. He tells the crowd, "As a school, I think we have to do more than teach about tolerance. I don't want to be tolerated, I want to be respected for who I am. A gay teenager."

In thinking about the work that the word "tolerance" does and doesn't do, I want to share what parent Maxime Redecopp (formerly Beausoleil) had to say about the difference between the words "tolerance," "acceptance," and "support" at school. Max is one of the parents interviewed in the *LGBTQ Families Speak Out* project (see Letter 12). In his interview, Max told us that he had lived with tolerance from his family all his life but didn't realize he could expect more than tolerance until he experienced acceptance and support from the LGBTQ community. For Max, "tolerance" means "Okay, well, I'll sit beside you." "Acceptance" means "I'll put my arm around you." But "support" means "I'll lift you up when you can't get up."[4]

Max believes teachers should talk to their students about the differences between "tolerance," "acceptance," and "support," and how different each of these concepts feels to people and families who identify as LGBTQ. In *Snakes and Ladders,* Chris would agree. Chris wants to be respected in his school and he wants his teachers and principals to create a school culture that is more than just tolerant. In the letters that follow, some of the other parents who participated in the *LGBTQ Families Speak Out* project talk about what it takes to create schools that are accepting and supportive, schools that will lift their children up if they need it.

Unlike Chris, however, Anne believes it's okay to use the word "tolerance" if it "gets the job done". From Anne's perspective, Parent 1 is not yet ready (and may never be ready) to support a school initiative that promotes acceptance of LGBTQ lives. Talking about Anti-Racism and Pride Week as an activity that promotes tolerance, co-existing peacefully, and sitting next to each other without violence is a first step for her school, and a productive way to respond to Parent 1's religious concerns.

Turning now to the parents whose voices are absent from the school council meeting, we don't hear from parents such as Bob Byers, whose children identify as LGBTQ. We also don't hear from LGBTQ parents who are sending their children to Karen's school. There are several reasons why these parents may not have been at the meeting. They may have had to work. They may have had to take care of younger children at home. Or they may have decided it would be too painful to hear what parents such as Parent 1 had to say about their children and their families. When teachers ask the question "What will the parents say?", they are usually thinking about concerns from straight, cisgender parents raising straight, cisgender children (or children who they think will grow up to be straight and cisgender). They aren't thinking of parents who identify as LGBTQ or parents with children who identify as LGBTQ. These parents often have concerns about the hostile school culture their children have to navigate. In many school boards, teachers and principals are mandated by equity and safe-school policies to create school cultures that expect and welcome LGBTQ students and families. Supporting the development and growth of GSAs and organizing an Anti-Racism and Pride Week is one way to begin building an inclusive school culture. As Bob Byers says, policies need to be implemented.

All the best,
Tara

Notes

1 See Goldstein, Collins, and Halder, 2007.
2 See Goldstein, Collins, and Halder 2007, p.58.

3 The statistic of 30 percent of all youth suicides are undertaken by gay and lesbian youth was the statistic that was reported when the play was first written in 2004. More recently, in 2012, Egale Canada Human Rights Trust (ECHRT) launched the report from the first national LGBTQ Youth Suicide Prevention Summit. The report states, "LGBTQ youth are at significantly greater risk of suicide than their heterosexual and cisgender peers: 33% of LGB youth have attempted suicide in general, and 47% of trans youth have thought about suicide in the past year alone" (Dyck 2012). In the United States, evidence from the nationally representative 2015 Youth Risk Behavior Surveillance System (YRBSS) reported that more than 29 percent of LGB high-school students attempted suicide that year, compared to 6 percent of heterosexual students (Kann et al. 2016).

4 Max's ideas here have been used in a lot of different types of anti-oppression training. There is likely an original source for these ideas, but unfortunately I have not been able to trace that source.

LETTER 4
RELIGIOUS CONCERNS

Dear Teacher:

In my last two letters I talked about how establishing a GSA and organizing an event such as Anti-Racism and Pride Week can improve the school culture for LGBTQ and gender diverse students and families. But, what do you do if you are a teacher who wants to create an inclusive school culture for all your students, and have your own religious concerns about anti-homophobia education? I take up this question in this letter and the one that follows. In this letter I discuss scene 10 of *Snakes and Ladders* where student teacher Rahima, who identifies as Muslim, tells Roberto she's uncomfortable introducing the guest speakers from a community organization called Teens Educating and Confronting Homophobia (T.E.A.C.H.). In the next letter I discuss the struggle to establish Gay Straight Alliances in a Catholic and a Jewish school.

While Rahima doesn't believe LGBTQ people should be discriminated against, and wants to work towards creating a safer and more inclusive school, she doesn't think it's okay to be gay. She tells Roberto, "You can't be gay and Muslim." Roberto disagrees and says he knows people who are working out how to be gay and still follow the Islamic faith. However, Rahima doesn't want to talk about how some Muslims are opening up religious texts to new interpretations, so Roberto agrees to introduce the guest speakers from T.E.A.C.H. for her if she assists him in facilitating a workshop on homophobic and racist name-calling. Rahima agrees.

When teachers read and discuss scene 10, some are favourably impressed with the way Roberto negotiates a space for Rahima to take up one aspect of anti-homophobia work: challenging name-calling. Others aren't. In a 2004 interview about their reading of *Snakes and Ladders*, two teachers, Judy and Barb (pseudonyms), had this to say about Roberto's response to Rahima.[1]

JUDY: ... Rahima and Roberto, I was very interested in those two and the kinds of discussion they were engaged in ... The discussions they were having around religion and queerness and how those fit together and – it was interesting to me to see their relationship develop and the kinds of ways that Roberto was questioning Rahima. And I, I have respect for his negotiations with her and, and also I think for her, the way she was interacting with him in terms of stating where she was at, what she was uncomfortable with and yet also maintaining her relationship with him and – I think they, of all the characters, come to an interesting sort of, I'm, I'm not sure whether it's a compromise or just an interesting space of negotiating together and working together.

BARB: ... the one teacher who, or student teacher, I found really annoying ... I think she was, she was supposed to be, I don't remember her name but, just so not willing to, to listen and ... she didn't feel comfortable talking about it or introducing it because what if somebody thinks she is [accepting of homosexuality] and it's, like, "get over it," you know?

While Judy characterizes Roberto's offer to introduce the guest speakers from T.E.A.C.H. as a way to respect and accommodate Rahima's religious beliefs, Barb believes Rahima needs to address her religious homophobia. Like Judy and Barb, my colleagues at a conference on teacher education and social justice in 2004 had different things to say about how to respond to Rahima's religious concerns about some of the anti-homophobia education work at her school. My colleagues' names are also pseudonyms.

SAM: Roberto should have pushed Rahima more. Tell her she is being homophobic.

KRIS: Roberto handled it well. He told Rahima "you can be Muslim and gay." He told her about a group that was working it out. He made her think. He pushed her in a way that was appropriate, that acknowledged her strong beliefs.

NAN: But if she's not pushed even more, she'll think it's enough to stop the slurs and have gay friends. Just because you have Black friends, it doesn't mean you're an anti-racist.

JIM: I want to talk about the importance of having allies at school. Not all allies are perfect allies. Rahima is not a perfect ally for Roberto. But she's a good enough ally. In a school of teachers like John, Rahima is an important ally.

JESS: Roberto gives Rahima a safe space [to talk about anti-homophobia education] and an entry point for engagement. It's a small act of subversion. When it comes to divine values, people incline themselves towards the particular position of their community. Not all communities are ready to work with religious texts and open them up to interpretation.

In this discussion there is no clear consensus about Roberto's decision to introduce T.E.A.C.H. in exchange for Rahima facilitating a name-calling workshop with him. When teachers ask me what I would do if I were Roberto, I tell them I'd think about the work different responses might do at a particular school in a particular moment. For example, in Roberto and Rahima's school, Roberto's decision to introduce T.E.A.C.H. for Rahima moves Anti-Racism and Pride Week forward. It also contributes to Rahima's continuing journey as an anti-homophobia educator. Yet, at the same time, I believe Rahima's refusal to introduce the guest speakers from T.E.A. C.H. does reproduce religious homophobia at the school. It is something Roberto has to live beside at this moment in time. Is the cost of living beside religious homophobia overridden by the gains of a name-calling workshop co-facilitated by Rahima and Roberto? For me it is. But other educators might disagree.

What would you do if you were Roberto? What would you do if you were Rahima?

As you think about your answer to this question, it might be helpful to understand the Toronto District School Board's institutional position on religious accommodation and anti-homophobia education.[2] TDSB sees anti-homophobia education as human rights education and safe school education, and expects all students and teachers to engage in such education at their schools. TDSB doesn't see this expectation to be in conflict with its position on religious accommodation in its schools. Religious accommodations, such as the provision of school space for prayers and permission to wear religious head coverings at school, are made only if they don't infringe on the human rights of others. Roberto's offer to introduce the members of T.E.A.C.H. if Rahima co-facilitates an anti-homophobia/anti-racist name-calling activity allows Rahima to participate in Anti-Racism and Pride Week. It gives her a space to begin doing some work.

Before I close this letter I'd like to say that, while she isn't the only student teacher in the play who has concerns about participating in Anti-Racism and Pride Week, Rahima is the only character whose concerns are associated with a set of religious beliefs. Several readers have raised questions about the hypervisibility of Muslim concerns about anti-homophobia education in the play. They rightly argue that there are concerns about gender and sexuality education within many other religious groups. In the next letter I discuss the challenges two students faced when they tried to establish Gay Straight Alliances in their Catholic and Jewish high schools.

Several other readers of *Snakes and Ladders* have also rightly argued that it's problematic to have only one Muslim teacher with one particular set of religious beliefs represented in the play. Not all Muslims hold the same religious beliefs as Rahima. As well, the play doesn't represent those Muslim people who also identify as LGBTQ and are working to share their stories and advocate for change. For example, Samra Habib is a Toronto writer who began photographing queer Muslims in 2014. Samra launched a project on Tumblr called "Just Me and Allah" to showcase stories about the challenges of being queer and Muslim.[3] "Just Me and Allah" has evolved into a worldwide project, with participants from the United States and Europe. In total, Samra has shot about 40 subjects, and people have contacted her asking if they can take part. Talking about her project, Samra says, "For a lot of my subjects it's difficult not only to find acceptance in traditional Muslim spaces, but to also fight against non-Muslim perceptions of what Muslim experiences are. My intention was to give queer Muslims a platform to share their own stories in their own words." To read five stories from Samra's series, go to https://torontolife.com/city/life/five-moving-stories-like-queer-muslim/.

All the best,

Tara

Notes

1 See Goldstein, 2004, for further discussion.
2 Copies of *Guidelines and Procedures for Religious Accommodations* are available at http://www.tdsb.on.ca/HighSchool/Equityinclusion/Guidelinespoli cies.aspx.
3 See Edwards, 2017, for further discussion of Samra Habib's project "Just Me and Allah." Samra is currently writing a memoir about her own experiences as a queer Muslim, called *We've Always Been Here*, which will be published in 2019 by Penguin Canada.

LETTER 5
FIGHTING FOR GSAS IN RELIGIOUS SCHOOLS

Dear Teacher:

In my last letter I discussed the activist work of writer Samra Habib, who created a project on Tumblr called "Just Me and Allah" that features a series of stories about queer Muslims. In this letter I want to introduce you to a high-school student named Lee Iskander, whose activism in their Catholic school helped create a law in Ontario that requires *all* government-funded schools in the province to establish a GSA if students request one. I also want to introduce you to Shulamit Izen, who, like Lee Iskander, fought to create a GSA in her Jewish high school in Boston.

In 2011 Lee Iskander identified as a White, lesbian, 16-year-old high school student, and attended a Catholic high school in Mississauga, a city west of Toronto. In March 2011, after a close friend was bullied at school, Lee and several other students at the school asked their principal for permission to start a Gay Straight Alliance.[1] Their request was denied. Instead, they were given pamphlets from Courage International, a Catholic organization which provides counselling to people who identify as lesbian, gay, and bisexual, so they could live chaste lives in accordance with the Roman Catholic Church's teaching on homosexuality.[2] The bullying continued.

In April, the students' request for a GSA was discussed by a group of Catholic school board trustees who decided they would allow "anti-bullying groups," but not groups who called themselves "Gay Straight Alliances." Lee wasn't satisfied. Lee, who uses the pronoun "they," believed students should be allowed to name their own groups. In an article published by the *Toronto Star*, Lee was quoted as saying:

We have to be able to name our groups. You can't censor our identity, which is essentially what they're doing. Words matter. It's like words are what bullying is [about] all of the time. It's very homophobic. So the name of the group definitely matters. I think publicly funded school systems including the Catholic system have a responsibility to be inclusive. I think they're really not being very accepting. It's really just a means of being not accepting.[3]

In June, Lee was named "Dyke and Youth Grand Marshal" for the annual Toronto Pride Parade which was to take place the following month.[4] They also won an *Inspire Award* for their activism. Despite this community recognition, Lee's school banned the use of rainbows (a symbol of LGBTQ pride) at the anti-homophobia day Lee and their classmates organized. To get around the ban, the students baked rainbow colours into the cupcakes they sold that day. Towards the end of June, just in time for the Pride Parade in July, Lee established a group called, Catholic Students for GSAs. The new coalition marched together in the parade.

In September, when school began again, the Toronto District Catholic School Board voted to put denominational rights ahead of human rights for all school board decisions, including decisions to grant students permission to establish support groups. Lee's second request to start a GSA in their school was denied again, and they were threatened with disciplinary action. Later that month Rick Mercer, a Canadian television personality, author, and comedian, took Catholic schools to task for banning GSAs during one of the "rants" on his weekly television show. Later that month, youth and adult activists, including teachers, held a rally to demand the Ontario provincial government, who is responsible for education policy, take action on the Catholic school boards' GSA ban.

In October, students in several other Catholic schools across Ontario requested permission to start GSAs in their schools. All of these requests were denied. Then, on October 20, 2011, a gay high school student in Ottawa, who had been trying to start a Rainbow Alliance at his school, committed suicide, and the issue of homophobic bullying in Ontario high schools began to dominate the news.

In November, the Ontario Liberal government put forward a new anti-bullying bill called the *Accepting Schools Act* for a first reading. In this reading the purpose of the *Accepting Schools Act (Bill 13)* was explained. The next day the Progressive Conservative opposition party put forward a competing *Anti-Bullying Bill (Bill 14)*. School bullying and Gay Straight Alliances were suddenly hot topics in the Ontario Legislative Assembly.

In January 2012, after the winter school break, Catholic students continued to fight for the right to establish GSAs in their schools. At the end of the month a group of Ontario bishops released a set of guidelines called "Respecting Difference," which provided a blueprint for establishing anti-bullying groups in Catholic schools. GSAs, however, were still banned.

In May, the *Accepting Schools Act* passed the second reading, where it was debated in principle, and then sent for review by committee. During a review by committee, public hearings can be held and amendments to a bill can be considered. The committee reviewing the *Accepting Schools Act* received a variety of public deputations, ranging from arguments by religious leaders to pleas for support from high school students. On May 25, 2012, a last-minute push by activists led to the addition of a new clause to the *Accepting Schools Act*, a clause that would mandate GSAs in all Ontario government-funded schools, including Ontario Catholic schools.

On June 5, 2012, just as the school year was about to end, Bill 13 passed the third reading. The *Accepting Schools Act* became law, creating legal obligations for school boards, elementary schools, and high schools to deliver tougher consequences for bullying. The law also stated that all government-funded schools in Ontario were required to establish GSAs and give students the power to name their own support groups.

There are two reasons I wanted to share this story of Lee Iskander's activist work to establish GSAs in Ontario Catholic schools. First, just like Lee, there are many students who believe their teachers and principals have a responsibility to create schools that are safe for all students, including those who identify as LGBTQ and those who come from LGBTQ families. If establishing a GSA helps accomplish this, and recent research shows it does (see Letter 2), then teachers and principals need to do whatever they can to create and support GSAs in their schools. Second, the story of Lee's activism shows it's possible for students to instigate change, even when it's difficult, and even when they are facing powerful religious doctrines, policies, and guidelines. Creating accepting schools involves creating new school cultures. Students, teachers, and principals can work together to build schools where LGBTQ students and families are expected, welcomed, supported, and feel like they belong.

You may be wondering what life is like for LGBTQ students and families in Ontario Catholic schools several years after the passing of the *Accepting Schools Act*. As you might imagine, people's experiences vary depending on the school they're attending. In some schools, students and teachers work together in clubs that have distinctive GSA names, such as Rainbow Alliance. In others, GSAs are part of larger groups that have names such as Respecting Difference and Open Arms. In some schools, principals and teachers monitor GSA groups to ensure that their discussions respect the *Pastoral Guidelines to Assist Students of Same-Sex Orientation*, written in 2004 for the Ontario Conference of Catholic Bishops. Because these guidelines characterize homosexuality as sinful and immoral, some students continue to feel unsafe, shamed, and humiliated at school. However, Mary Evered, a White, lesbian, Catholic school teacher in Toronto whose video interview appears on our *LGBTQ Families Speak Out* website, believes "We are seeing great changes with a much more enlightened Pope."[5] She tells us she's "been blown away in the last little while with certain changes that seem to be afoot: a greater sense of tolerance and openness and a recognition that everyone is a child of God."

Mary teaches in a Catholic school where the GSA has been established for a number of years. The group is called Dialogue and was started by the head of the Religion Department. Mary believes it was the first GSA to be established in any Catholic school in Ontario. There are a number of teachers involved in Dialogue, both gay and straight, and the group has been involved in a lot of activism over the years. Yet Mary knows her own GSA experience is not widely shared. She told us of the time she accompanied Dialogue to a meeting sponsored by EGALE, a Canadian non-profit organization whose tagline is "Progress Through Inclusion." The organization works to improve the lives of LGBTQ people in Canada through research, education, and community engagement and was the sponsor of research on Canadian school climates discussed in Letter 2. At the meeting, which was an attempt to bring GSAs from different Catholic schools together to share experiences, Mary learned that teachers who participated in GSAs at other schools were not as well supported as the teachers in her school were. She told us that one teacher didn't get permission from her principal to come to the EGALE meeting, and she had taken a sick day to participate. This teacher's students didn't get permission to participate either. Their parents had to call them in sick as well. So, the work to establish and sustain GSAs in Catholic schools continues. While students and teachers have the legal right to establish a GSA in their Catholic schools, not all principals support them.

Like Lee Iskander, Shulamit Izan, a high school student at an independent Jewish school in Boston, also faced religious opposition when she asked her principal, Rabbi Lehmann, to establish a GSA at their school. The story of Shulamit's activism is told in an engaging documentary film produced in 2005 called *Hineini: Coming Out in a Jewish High School* and directed by Irena Fayngold.[6] "Hineini" is Hebrew for "here I am."

The documentary is made up of interviews with Shulamit, her family, teachers, and Rabbi Lehmann, as well as other students who both support and oppose creating a GSA at their school. In the film, Irena Fayngold focuses on the challenge of addressing tensions between religious pluralism and sexual diversity in religious schools and shows how Rabbi Lehmann comes to understand that the core of Jewish tradition is to bring together conflicting opinions, "not in an attempt to somehow resolve them or create harmony, but to actually live in the tension of those differences."[7] I find the idea of not expecting to resolve religious differences, but finding ways to live in the tension of opposing views, very helpful. It provides religious schools, who are legally responsible for providing support for their LGBTQ students and families, with a way forward. It is an idea that helped Roberto and Rahima in *Snakes and Ladders* find a way to work together during Anti-Racism and Pride Week.

All kinds of discussions about LGBTQ inclusion, from sanctifying same-sex marriages to ordaining LGBTQ rabbis, ministers, and priests, are currently taking place in many religious institutions. In the next letter, Kevin Robertson, an Anglican bishop and gay parent, talks about the ways he and his family live in the tension of opposing views on whether or not his family have the right to belong in the Anglican Church.

All the best,

Tara

Notes

1 For a documented timeline of these events, see Houston, A. (2012) "Mission Accomplished," *Xtra!* (Toronto), June 14, 2012.

2 For an explanation of the Roman Catholic Church's teaching on homosexuality, see the Ontario Conference of Catholic Bishops (2004) *Pastoral Guidelines to Assist Students of Same-Sex Orientation.* Toronto: Ontario Conference of Catholic Bishops. Available on the Assembly of Catholic Bishops of Ontario website: http://acbo.on.ca/englishdocs/Pastoral%20Guidelines.pdf.

3 Zerbisias, A. (2012) "Gay Straight Alliances Save Lives Say Ontario Students," *The Toronto Star*, June 1, 2012.

4 The word "dyke" is used to refer to people who identify as lesbians. Historically it was used as a slur, but recently has been reclaimed by some lesbians who use it to name themselves.

5 Interview, March 11, 2015.

6 See Fayngold, 2005.

7 Fayngold, 2005.

LETTER 6

LOVE

Dear Teacher:

In my last letter I discussed the activism of two high-school students, Lee Iskander and Shulamit Izan, who established GSAs in their Catholic and Jewish schools. I also discussed the way Shulamit's principal, Rabbi Lehmann, asked the teachers, students, and parents in his school to live in the tension between their own religious beliefs about gender and sexuality and his students' request for a GSA. In this letter I want to share what Anglican Bishop Kevin Robertson and his partner Mohan Sharma, as out gay parents, had to say about living beside conservative religious beliefs held by some members in the Anglican Church while raising their children.

Kevin is the bishop of 58 Anglican parishes and missions in Toronto. He identifies as White, gay, cisgender, and Anglican. Mohan's parents were born in India and Denmark. While his father identifies as Hindu and his mother as Lutheran, Mohan went to Catholic school and often attends Anglican church services with Kevin. Mohan identifies as mixed-race, gay, and cisgender.

KEVIN: I was an Anglican priest before I was a bishop, and that's the way things work in the Anglican Church. Bishops in our Church are elected. And so I served 20 years in a parish – not all of that out, but I came out during that time. And this also will be a long story, the history of the Anglican Church, and its own homophobia, and its own coming to terms – only 25 years ago, a priest in our diocese was fired for being in a relationship with another man – a male priest in a relationship with another man. So, we've been through a turbulent 25 years, we're in a way, way better place than we were, but the changes have come pretty quickly. So, when I was elected bishop, Mohan and I have been together for nine years. And I was elected just a year ago, so certainly by the time my name was on the ballot, and in the last parish I served, I mean, obviously everybody knew about our relationship, about our kids, and about our family construct, and so my election was somewhat controversial. There were people who objected to me being on the ballot because I'm gay, or openly gay. I mean, my goodness, we've probably had hundreds and hundreds of gay bishops in the Church over the last 2,000 years, but the fact that I was out, and that we were out, and we were raising a family together in an unconventional way, there were certainly some clergy who felt that should disqualify me from being – even being on the ballot.

I happen to think that their objections helped me get elected, because there were people in the senate that day who were so outraged by this homophobia that I suspect that I probably got some votes from some people who maybe didn't even know me that well, but thought "I'm going to vote for that guy because other people don't want him to get elected."

Anyway, I was elected and became the first openly gay bishop in the Anglican Church of Canada, and I was appointed as the area bishop for an area called York-Scarborough, which is downtown, North Toronto, North York, the east end of the city, and Scarborough, so I have kind of the urban part of our diocese – of the Diocese of Toronto.[1] And so, I've been in that role for just over a year. I was selected in September 2016, and then consecrated a bishop just a year ago this month. So, I've had 12 months of that, and we've had 12 months of adjusting to what that is like.

Our kids were very funny because, you know, I wore a black shirt for a while [when Kevin was a priest], and then I started wearing a purple shirt – and they were at the consecration [the ordaining of Kevin as a bishop] obviously, and things like that – but they think it's kind of funny that I wear different clothes, and I wear a pointy hat now, and a purple shirt.

And, uh, so one of the – one of the things about being a pioneer in this way is that I'm a pioneer at work and face the joys and the challenges of that, but it carries over into our home life, and our kids' lives, and their school life as well. So, dropping the kids off and picking them up and parents, teachers, and the school staff seeing us together with our kids, seeing me dressed like this, and you can just tell they are trying to make sense out of this. Especially – especially those who have come from a religious background, like maybe Roman Catholics, or more conservative Anglicans, or Pentecostals, whatever. They identify this [indicating his outfit and cross] with Christianity, and many people identify Christianity with conservatism, and they just can't compute about how that [Kevin's LGBTQ family] can be a part of this.

MOHAN: As we're dropping the kids off, or picking them up, you see people looking at us. They see the collar, and they often see us together with the kids, or they know the kids, and they will look at us and you can tell that the wheels are going, they're trying to figure things out.

But, you know, as much as that happens, there's also people trying to understand it. Shortly after Kevin became a bishop, there was a story [journalist] Michael Corrin did, it was in *The Toronto Star*, and then the following Monday we were taking the kids to school and – I wasn't there but you [looking at Kevin] told me this – he walked in, and immediately as you walk in the school, the office, the school office, is on the left-hand side, and the entire office, the principal, the vice-principal, the secretary, the admin staff, they all got up and they clapped, and they came out and gave Kevin a big hug. And so, although there are people who don't know, there are people who do. And it was – I got goosebumps, I wasn't even there, Kevin told me about it after the fact. So, there's that joy, that openness, and understanding, and acceptance that we've received so lovingly by strangers. So, it's been lovely.

KEVIN: I also think that in our – our society is becoming rapidly secularized, and I think in some ways that actually makes it easier for me, which would be – it sounds like a strange thing to say. But I think the fact that lots of people are not as attached to a particular set of religious convictions in the way they once were. I mean, if I had been an openly gay – well, I wouldn't have been an openly gay bishop 50 years ago, but imagine I was – and then walked into our kids' school, I think I'd be faced with lots of scorn and, like, judgement, because people in those days held their religious convictions – lots of people held their religious convictions quite closely. And I just don't think that's the case anymore. I think in many religious organizations, including in many churches, and certainly in secular society, people are much more open to different and new things, which I think is good. Really good.

TARA: Right. Going back to the, um, bumper sticker [the bumper sticker Kevin and Mohan picked up while they were on vacation in Provincetown, Massachusetts]: "Jesus had two dads and it all kind of worked out . . ."

MOHAN: [Correcting Tara] "He turned out all right."

TARA: Yeah, "He turned out all right", which is just a fantastic bumper sticker. When folks do talk to you about what they see to be the contradictions between being faithful and, uh, having an LGBTQ family, what are some of the things that you say? Do you find yourself getting involved in those conversations, or do you prefer not to get involved in those conversations?

KEVIN [TO MOHAN]: Do you want to field this or . . .?

MOHAN: Well, we haven't – I don't think that we've been – people might have those views, but they haven't challenged us. They haven't, or I can't recall that happening. I mean, if somebody were to say that to us . . . for me, I would say that if there is a teaching that Jesus taught us, it's love, and it's love, and it's love. And us loving each other and loving our kids, I mean, there is no inconsistency. There is no inconsistency, and that's all I would have to say.

KEVIN: I would say, in my professional world I certainly get challenged about that, not always overtly, but even somebody standing up the day of my election to say that I shouldn't be elected. Those people, the people – not those people – the people who stood up to make the objection rested their objection on a set of biblical and theological principles and understanding. So, they would – I would certainly have been in theological and biblical conversations about reconciling our life together and our life with our kids with a more traditional Christian understanding. Absolutely. And I think that's nothing new. I think that, in fact, even in places like the Roman Catholic

Church, the LGBTQ voice is being heard like it's never been heard before, and the hierarchy there and in other churches, including the Anglican Church, which had either suppressed that or ignored it, can't do that anymore. Like, we're just in a completely different space ...

... I think churches, certain churches anyway, are grappling with this, and doing something about it, because of where we are and where we've been in relation to society. I do think it's a – I do think it's related to power. Most things are related to power in some way, right? And I think there's some truth to the fact that mainline churches have lost so much in the last 25 to 50 years. Lost a lot of people, lost buildings, lost the, the currency of influence in – with government and society. You know, there was a time when the Anglican Church was basically the state church in Canada. We weren't the biggest church, but we were the church of prime ministers, and premiers, and judges, and mayors. And, that's not as true as it used to be, and I think the loss of influence and the loss of power has led us into a place of greater vulnerability, and that seems like a loss for a lot of church-goers; and it is in one sense, but it's also a huge gain to be less tethered to government, to civic society, to business. It sets the church free, I think, to be something different, and the – what I was saying a few moments ago, 25 years ago a priest in our diocese was fired for being in a same-sex relationship, and now ... here I am, an openly gay bishop with my partner, only in 25 years, but I think it's a sign of the Church's need to recreate itself ...

... I have 58 parishes in my area of the diocese ... There are 58 parishes and missions, and I've been to – by the end of March I will have been to ... 55. I will have not been to the other three, because, frankly, I'm not really welcomed there. Now, I'm the bishop, so I have a right to be there, but we are still in conversation about what that's going to look like. They're the three most conservative parishes, and I would have hoped that, a year in, people in our Anglican Church in the diocese would have said "All right, we've got an openly gay bishop with a partner and two kids, it – let's just move on." And for the most part I think they have, really. But in a couple of places there are still people who are, like, "I'm not accepting the leadership and ministry of a gay bishop." I'm not sure they would say that in the words that I have just used, but it's abundantly clear when I say, "I'm going to visit your parish on such-and-such a Sunday," [they respond with] "Well, you know, I'm not sure, you know. I think we need to have a conversation about that." So, there is – in some pockets – there is still, still some resistance, if I can use that analogy. And that's discouraging. I know change takes time, and I do believe changes have happened relatively quickly in our Church, so I'm not – this isn't sour grapes. I'm really grateful – but the work is not yet done. And I would say the work is not yet done in schools, even though we've had a great experience, we're at a particularly good place, because we have such a great school, such great teachers, but I imagine that that's not the case everywhere, so I think we've got tons of work to do in society, in schools, in the Church, to make those places safe places for everyone.

In his interview, Kevin says he believes he is part of a new moment in the Anglican Church of Canada – a moment where an out gay man raising children with his out gay partner can be elected bishop of 58 parishes. However, he also acknowledges that three of his 58 parishes won't invite him to participate in their Sunday services despite his authority as bishop of their diocese. Like Mary Evered in Letter 5, Kevin believes there is still work to be done before the Anglican Church is truly inclusive. Nevertheless, he and his partner Mohan are able to live beside the religious homophobia they sometimes experience because they have the support of most of Kevin's parishioners, and support from the staff at their children's school. One of Mohan's strategies for responding to moments of homophobia is lightly remarking that Jesus had two fathers and he turned out all right. The other is reminding people that Jesus preached love. Mohan believes that the love he and Kevin have for each other and their children is an example of the love Jesus preached.

Elementary school teacher and teacher educator benjamin lee hicks has also written about the importance of love. For hicks, in order to create schools that truly expect, welcome, and support LGBTQ families and students, teachers need to build loving communities in their classrooms.[2] When hicks, who uses the pronoun "they," writes about loving communities, they are thinking about the explicit teaching of love that writer bell hooks discusses in her book *All About Love: New Visions*.[3] hooks, drawing from M. Scott Peck (echoing Erich

Fromm), understands love as "the will to extend one's self for the purpose of nurturing one's own or another's spiritual growth." To create a loving, nurturing community in their own classroom, at the beginning of the school year, hicks asked their students to create a set of agreements that brought the principles of love, respect, inclusion, and peace-full resolution to life in their classroom.[4] Here are the four examples (of several more) classroom agreements hicks and the students created around the principle of love at Palmerston Avenue Public School in 2010–2011:

- We believe that our classroom is a microcosm of the world and that we have a lot of control over the balance of hate and compassion within our small community.
- We will be compassionate and give everyone the chances that they need to make positive change so that they can earn more trust within the group.
- We agree that everyone deserves a clean slate every day, and that this is one way that we can increase LOVE.
- We consciously choose to increase the amount of love in our class, which will directly reduce the amount of hate. We believe that love is an antidote for hate.

While it may seem unusual to talk about what love looks like in an elementary (or secondary) school classroom, learning to care for one another with skill and action is what it takes to build an inclusive school culture that expects, welcomes, and supports LGBTQ students and families.

All the best,
Tara

Notes

1 A diocese is a district under the pastoral care of a bishop in the Christian Church.
2 See hicks, 2017.
3 See hooks, 2000.
4 For a list of the classroom agreements around the principles of respect, inclusion, and peace-full resolution, see hicks, 2017.

PART 2
GENDER AT SCHOOL

LETTER 7
GENDER, GENDER IDENTITY, AND GENDER EXPRESSION

Dear Teacher:

To begin this section on gender at school I want to offer some introductory remarks about gender, gender identity, and gender expression by turning to a book my students and I have really enjoyed reading together. It's called *The Gender Book*, and it is written as a coloured comic book with hand-drawn graphics and captions.[1]

Mel Reiff Hill and Jay Mays, the authors of *The Gender Book*, begin their exploration into gender by starting with what they think their readers already know. I quote them extensively here to give you an opportunity to take stock of what you already know about gender, gender identity, and gender expression.

> You probably have the idea that gender is somehow connected to your body parts or DNA, you might think of gender as having something to do with sexuality, you probably have heard of intersex people, and of course you are fluent in the gender roles of the culture you grew in ... Additionally, you may know that not everyone fits these roles, and that surgeries exist to help those who feel very uncomfortable in the bodies they were born with. If you watch television, you may have heard of Chaz Bono or the man who was pregnant or seen beautiful women on daytime TV shows that "have a secret". You know on your government forms there are only two options for gender (unless you live in Nepal), and that even your doctor uses the words "gender" and "sex" interchangeably. You probably also know that bullying is a real

49

problem for boys who are too feminine or other kids who don't fit traditional roles.[2]

After describing some of the things they think their readers may already know, Reiff Hill and Mays move on to examine which of these things are true and which may be common misconceptions. Here, in their words, are several misconceptions people often have about gender.

1. Gender is the same as sex.

> No way! Maybe it matches for you, but not everyone feels that way. The short answer is that sex is in your body while gender is in your mind.[3]

> While gender refers to your identity and the expression of that identity (which can include your relationship to your body), sex is a label that refers strictly to your body – specifically to the reproductive organs, DNA, chromosomes, and hormone-dependent characteristics like body hair and breast tissue.[4]

> When you go to a new doctor, she might ask you if you are male or female and check a box: that's your sex marker. You'll see it on driver's licenses and birth certificates. Most people's bodies correspond to one of the standard (M/F) markers but not everyone's.[5]

2. There are only two genders.

> This misconception is so common it has its own name – the gender binary. Actually, there are (at least) as many genders as there are cultures, and lots of more helpful ways to think of them than simply masculine and feminine.[6]

> Many societies throughout time and across the globe have had additional or intermediary gender roles co-existing with their versions of masculinity and femininity.[7]

3. Body parts have significance.

> Just because most women have breasts doesn't mean everyone with breasts is a woman (for example), or that a woman without them is any less a woman. The same is true for any body part.[8]

4. Gender is obvious.

> Nope! The only way to be sure you know how someone identifies is to ask them.[9]

5. Gender is static.

> Your understanding of gender can evolve as you do![10]

Having clarified that there are more than two genders (male and female), sex and gender are not the same thing, and not everyone feels comfortable with the gender they were assigned at birth, Reiff Hill and Mays go on to discuss a variety of gender identities that are available to people and a variety of ways people can express their gender. Before moving on to a discussion of gender identity and gender expression, however, I'd like to discuss the differences between gender and sexual orientation. Sexual orientation is about our romantic and/or sexual attractions to people of a specific gender or genders. For example, a person who identifies as a man (regardless of the sex assigned to him at birth) who is mostly attracted to women probably identifies as straight or heterosexual. If that same attraction to women was from a person who identifies as female, she may identify as a lesbian. But, as Reiff Hill and Mays remind us, you never know. Every person decides which words feel right to describe themselves. In thinking about all the possibilities that exist in romance, Reiff Hill and Mays write:

- Anyone of any gender can be attracted to anyone else of any gender(s).
- Anyone of any gender can be anywhere from asexual to very sexual.
- Anyone of any gender can be with anywhere from zero to multiple partners.

Understanding this was very helpful when my research team and I started interviewing LGBTQ families about their experiences at school.

Gender Identity and Gender Expression

When babies are born, people have expectations about what they're going to be like based on their sex. If a baby has a penis, he is called a boy and is often wrapped in a blue baby blanket. If a baby has a vagina, she is called a girl and is wrapped in a pink blanket. A baby's assigned gender is then reinforced through their lifetime in a number of ways; for example, when people buy them toys and clothes. By the time a baby becomes a toddler, they already have a sense of their her (assigned) gender identity and begin to make connections between their anatomy and gender roles. My own earliest memory of my gender identity is captured in a photo of me in a very feminine dress with a purple velvet top and a white, puffy crinoline skirt. I'm wearing white ankle socks and black patent leather shoes with straps. I started life as a very feminine girl. But, like many other people, the way I choose to express my gender identity has changed over the years. As an adult I very rarely wear a dress or a skirt, and prefer to dress in pants and a jacket or blazer.

When children begin school they are already very good at making decisions about their gender expression or gender performance, based on what they've learned from friends, family, TV shows, and games. Other children, teachers, and parents often reinforce these roles, making comments such as "You can't skip rope, that's a girl's game." Gender rules can be very rigid and limiting. By offering children more options for gender self-expression and showing children that there are many ways to be a girl or a boy, or both or neither, teachers can address gender-based harassment and bullying; for example, girls not being allowed to play hockey or soccer with the boys during recess, or boys being teased or harassed for wearing pink or playing with dolls.

The Gender Binary and the Gender Spectrum
The "gender binary" is the name given to the belief system that there are only two genders: male and female. In this system, people are either male or female and their gender and sex are assumed to be the same thing. However, this isn't true for many people who identify on a spectrum of gender diversity (see the entries for "genderqueer," "gender fluid," "gender independent," and "gender creative" in "The Unicorn Glossary").

A person who identifies as transgender is a person whose sense of their gender identity is different from the biological sex that they were assigned at birth. The Latin prefix "trans" that appears before the word "gender" in transgender means "the other side of." In contrast, the Latin prefix "cis" that appears before the word "gender" in the word "cisgender" means "the same side of." So, a person who identifies as cisgender is someone whose gender identity and expression match the social expectations for the physical/biological sex they were assigned at birth. Sex assignment is based on a (binary) medical perception of people's sex chromosomes, gonads, reproductive chromosomes, and external genitalia.

The term "intersex" is a general term applied to a variety of situations in which a person who is born with a reproductive or sexual anatomy that doesn't seem to fit the typical medical definitions of female or male. For example, a person might be born appearing to be female on the outside but actually has mostly male-typical anatomy on the inside.

"Genderqueer," "gender fluid," and "non-binary" are relatively recent terms, and are mostly used by people who experience a very fluid sense of their gender identity and sexual orientation. People who identify as genderqueer, gender fluid, and non-binary do not want to be constrained by absolute or static gender and/or sexual identities. They prefer to be open to locating themselves on continuums of gender and sexual orientation.

"Gender independent" and "gender creative" are also terms that are used to refer to children whose gender identity and/or gender expression differ from what is culturally expected from someone of their assigned sex. For example, in the animated video *Tomboy*, a 9-year-old named Alex (short for Alejandra) loves playing soccer but is harassed by her classmates for acting more like a boy than like a girl.[11] In a nasty exchange during a soccer game, one of the classmates tells Alex to get off the field and find a pretty dress to wear. It is a humiliating and frustrating moment for Alex, and she runs home in tears. Fortunately, Alex has support at home. When her mother finds her up in her bedroom crying, she comforts Alex and reassures her she's great just the way she is.

An alternative system to the gender binary system is the gender spectrum or the gender continuum, which imagines infinite genders ranging from the very masculine on one side of the spectrum or continuum to the very feminine on the other side. When I wore my purple velvet dress as a little girl, my gender identity could be read as sitting at the very feminine side of the spectrum. When Alex wears red shorts to school and plays soccer with the boys at recess, she is read by others as sitting closer to the masculine side of the spectrum. But, no one can know the full truth of another person's gender identity just by looking at the way they express themselves externally. This is especially true when we are reading people through the lens of binary gender ideas that many people – including many gender creative kids – do not thrive within. Teachers who understand this and expect gender diversity among their students are prepared to serve their students well.

All the best,

Tara

Notes

1 See Reiff Hill and Mays, 2013.
2 See Reiff Hill and Mays, 2013, p.1.
3 See Reiff Hill and Mays, 2013, p.2.
4 See Reiff Hill and Mays, 2013, p.8.
5 See Reiff Hill and Mays, 2013, p.8.
6 See Reiff Hill and Mays, 2013, p.2.
7 See Reiff Hill and Mays, 2013, p.6.
8 See Reiff Hill and Mays, 2013, p.2.
9 See Reiff Hill and Mays, 2013, p.2.
10 See Reiff Hill and Mays, 2013, p.2.
11 See Taylor and Pendleton Jiménez, 2008.

LETTER 8

GENDER PRONOUNS

Dear Teacher:

Before I met any transgender or genderqueer people, I believed there were only two genders and people only used the pronouns "she"/"her" or "he"/"him" to describe themselves. When I found out that some people use gender-neutral pronouns such as "they"/"them"/"their" – as in "Alex is a good friend so I took them to a movie for their birthday" – it took me a while to get used to. Gender-neutral or gender-inclusive pronouns like they/them/their don't refer to one particular gender. So, when I use a gender-neutral pronoun to talk about someone, it allows me not to label or associate them with a specific gender. I've learned this is very important to people who identify with multiple genders, or even no gender at all. My colleague Lee Airton has this to say about what it means to them to use "they" as their pronoun.

> I'm a long-time user of the gender-neutral pronoun, singular "they." I ask that others use this familiar standard English pronoun when referring to me because it doesn't put me in either the man or woman basket. Why? Because a lifetime of abiding gender non-conformity has led me to a place where singular "they" makes deep sense. I have found that it facilitates my ability to be myself and in the world, where I commit my energy and enthusiasm to doing the best that I can for myself, my students, and my communities . . .
>
> . . . I'll be the first to admit that my pronoun can be silly sometimes, that it can cause confusion, prompting the need for clarification. It takes patience, practice, and sometimes humour.

But I've found over the years that working through these little challenges can foster warmth, connection, and community.[1]

In the spirit of fostering warmth, connection, and community in our Sexualities, Gender, and Schooling course, my students and I usually start off every class with a name and pronoun check. Each student reminds the group of their name and what pronoun they use. The name and pronoun check is also useful for introducing the members of the class to guest speakers, who then also have an opportunity to let us know what pronouns they use. Even with a name and pronoun check at the beginning of each class, I still sometimes make a mistake and use the wrong pronoun when talking to my students or colleagues. When I do, I apologize and correct myself. Getting my students' and colleagues' pronouns right is a sign of respect.

During our name and pronoun check, some of the students will tell the class what pronoun they "prefer"; for example, "I prefer she/her." Others will tell us what pronoun they "use"; for example, "I use they/them." In thinking about the difference between saying "I prefer" and "I use", I've come to realize that, for some people, the pronouns they use are not preferred, they are mandatory.

Of all the gender-neutral pronouns I've learned about, they/them seem to be the most common. But, here are some other ones:

- "ze/hir" as in "Ze walks hir dog twice a day."
- "phe/per" as in "Phe named per dog Biscuit."
- "thon/thon" as in "Thon takes thon's dog to the park every afternoon."
- "ey/em" as in "Ey went to the park, and I went with em."[2]

If you're interested in learning more about using gender-neutral pronouns, Lee Airton's blog *They is My Pronoun* is an excellent place to begin.[3] Airton has been using "they" as their personal pronoun since 2011 and has been writing their blog since 2012. Their motivation for creating the blog came from their own everyday experiences of using the pronouns they, them, and they. Interesting blog entries for teachers include "The honest mistake: On being a pronoun beginner," "Singular they and verb conjugation," and "Are gender-neutral pronouns a white people thing?" I've really enjoyed following Lee's blog and I think you will too.

All the best,
Tara

Notes

1 See Airton, 2016.
2 See Reiff Hill and Mays, 2013, p.16.
3 See http://www.theyismypronoun.com.

LETTER 9
TRANSITIONING IN GRADE 1

Dear Teacher:

In this letter, I want share the experience of 6-year-old Violet Addley (a pseudonym) who transitioned from a boy to a girl in Grade 1. My research team and I first met Violet and the Addley family (a pseudonym) in the spring of 2015 when we interviewed them for our research study on the experiences of LGBTQ families in Ontario schools. As I discussed in my "Getting Acquainted" letter, the goals of the study are to interview LGBTQ families about their experiences at school, document how families have worked with schools to create safer and more respectful classrooms for their children, and share the families' interviews with teachers and principals so they can begin to think about the ways they can best work with LGBTQ students and families.

What follows are several excerpts from the Addley family's interview with the research team. There are three parents and four children in the family, and they all identify as White. While Violet identifies transgender, all the others identify as cisgender. Ms. Richards (a pseudonym), Violet's teacher, also identifies as White and cisgender.

SARA (A PSEUDONYM) (PARENT): We are a family of seven.

MAY (A PSEUDONYM) (PARENT): Yes. Three parents. We call ourselves polyfidelitious.

SARA: You can google it.

MAY: This is as far as the family, the family goes. No more kids. No more adults. This is the core, this is us. Um, yeah, we, uh, I'm at home with the kids. I, uh, volunteer at the school and I have a little job there as a lunchroom supervisor. So I'm there constantly. And I love it. And, uh, try to infiltrate the system with as much positive trans stuff as I possibly can. Fielding a lot of questions for, for Violet . . .

***

JON (A PSEUDONYM) (PARENT): . . . [We decided] we need[ed] a positive experience to put under the transgender cone.

MAY: It was just after she became Violet. So I found out there was the first trans flag raising at [Toronto] City Hall. So I thought, you know, this is perfect. So we got all fancied up, and we went down, and we saw the flag go up. And we saw other trans people who were, like, encouraging her . . . They wrapped her in the flag! . . . And she, uh, we arrived at City Hall and she said "We're going to a flag raising, because I'm transgender!" And it was the first time she said it out loud! And I'm like, I could feel it coming out, "You don't have to!" But I didn't, I was just like, "I'm proud of you! You're so –" You know! Because it was, it was great, it was just weird for me. So we did that, and, uh, you know, we're leaving and she's looking back and she's seeing that flag that represents her, and she's like, "We should come back tomorrow and see it!"

***

MAY: When it first happened, Violet was like, "Can I just have an assembly and tell everyone?" because she just did not want to ask or, like, answer any more questions.

SARA: That bugged her a lot.

MAY: Questions, questions, questions.

SARA: People asking the same thing every day.

MAY: Every day was just getting more – so I took an active role because they [Jon and Sara] make the money but they encourage me to, uh, to volunteer, like in her class . . . and then I'm in all different kinds of classes . . . as lunchroom supervisor . . . So I'm getting the questions. Which is awesome. Because then they don't ask her . . .

***

MAY: . . . [Y]ou could always tell, uh, she liked all different kinds of things. And [her teacher] Ms. Richards kind of took her under her wing, and, um, every time it was time for her to just start a new class, Ms. Richards would say "I'm taking her with me. I'm going to the next grade." And, uh, when Violet wanted to wear her Elsa dress for the first time to school, I didn't have the guts to do it, but I sent it in her bag, and Ms. Richards put it in – put her in it . . . And she called and said, "She's in it now, she's in it now!" And I was like, "Oh my God, what's happening? Is it okay?" But she was the one to really have, like, the guts. And then I thought from that point on, "Oh my gosh, I need to up my game here . . ."

. . . I would buy dresses but they were pyjama dresses . . . So you know, I was putting my own kind of labels of what was okay . . .

. . . You know, I never anticipated that she would become Violet. I just thought, you know, she's a boy who wears pink. But I think upping the game is just questioning ourselves at all these little points that we are blocking her from being herself.

SARA: Not worrying about [what] other people are saying.

MAY: Yes. Because that's the fear. If you wear a dress and you feel great in front of the mirror, and you feel different leaving, that's, like, that's not okay. You know, you have to know you felt good in my safe place, and outside is safe too . . . [R]ight now, she's got confidence. And all we gotta do is keep it. Raise it up.[1]

In her conversation about the kind of advocacy she has engaged in at Violet's school, May talks about the importance of fielding questions for Violet. As a part-time lunch supervisor and volunteer at her children's school, May has worked hard to create a school culture that is accepting and supportive of Violet. She's created relationships with Violet's schoolmates and is available to answer their questions about Violet's transition. In discussing her own process of becoming comfortable with Violet's transition, May talks about the importance of Ms. Richards' allyship and how Ms. Richards' confidence helped May find the confidence to send Violet to school in a dress. Confidence is key. As May notes, right now Violet has the confidence to be whoever she wants to be. It's her family's and teacher's job to make sure Violet keeps that confidence and increases it.

While Ms. Richards' work was vital in helping Violet socially transition, May also received support from a member of her school board's equity team who helped Violet change her name on her school records. When he began working with the Addley family, the Equity and Inclusive Education Student/Community Facilitator helped them come up with a plan. May says, "I remember him asking 'What do you want? What are you hoping to see for her?'"[2] May also credits the receptive principal who invited the equity facilitator to the school to support the family. Having this kind of institutional support made Violet's legal transition possible.

In thinking about what made Violet's transition in school so successful, I want to return to the Triangle Model, the analytical framework I discussed in my "Getting Acquainted" letter. I learned about the Triangle Model from participating in numerous anti-racist education workshop in the early 1990s. The Triangle Model sees experiences of oppression and discrimination as falling into three different categories – ideas, individual practices, and institutional practices. Breaking down the cycle of oppression involves changing all three ways that people experience it.

Ms. Richards' individual action of encouraging Violet to wear a dress at school is connected to her understanding that gender is not the same as sex. While her own gender matches her sex, Ms. Richards knows that not everyone feels the same way she does. She understands that Violet feels like a girl even though she was assigned male at birth. Because Ms. Richards used her authority to make it safe enough for Violet to wear a dress in her classroom, Violet was able to begin *socially* transitioning at school. Because there was institutional support from the board's Equity and Inclusive Education Student/Community Facilitator and a receptive principal, Violet was able to *legally* transition as well. There is much to learn from Violet's experience of transitioning at school, and in the next letter I will discuss what some of the teachers enrolled in our Sexualities, Gender, and Schooling course said they took away from the Addley family's interview.

All the best,
Tara

Notes

1 Interview, June 15, 2015.
2 Interview, June 15, 2015.

LETTER 10
TEACHER ALLYSHIP

Dear Teacher:

In the Sexualities, Gender, and Schooling course offered in the fall of 2016, graduate students, Austen Koecher and benjamin lee hicks, and I provided our students with the option to write about what they learned from the Addley family interviews in their final assignment. The assignment was designed to provide the teachers with an opportunity to do some self-analysis and self-reflection about the experiences LGBTQ families have in school. Here is the description of the assignment.

Final Assignment, Option 1: LGBTQ Families' Experiences in School

Examine and respond to the video interview clips of three individuals or families posted on lgbtqfamiliesspeakout.ca

In this assignment you can build upon your work with the video clips from earlier in the course, or work with new videos. Start by watching all of the clips for three (or more) individuals or families. While you watch, think about the questions below. After you watch the videos, answer the following questions, comparing and contrasting between the experiences of the three individuals or families.

1. Think about a moment in the videos that resonated with your own experience. In what ways, if any, did it resonate with something in your own life or the life of someone you know?

If there were no moments in the videos that resonated with your own experience, write about a moment that surprised you and why.

2. Think about a moment in the videos that provoked an emotional response for you. What was it and why do you think that you responded emotionally to that moment?

3. Thinking of the experiences of the participants in the videos you watched, what is important for teachers and other educators to know about? What can educators learn from these experiences?

4. What are you taking away from the videos? How might this inform your future practice?

You can choose how much space to dedicate to each of the four questions, but you should answer them all. If it helps you to reflect on the experiences of the participants, you can choose to relate your responses to our course readings, but this is not required.

Not all of the students chose this option, and of those that did, not all of them chose to write about the Addley interviews. Some wrote about the interviews we did with other LGBTQ families. However, several teachers reflected on what they learned from the Addley family, and in this letter I want to share what two of them said.

After watching the Addley family video clips, Teacher 1 wrote about how some children, even at a very young age, are aware that their gender identity is different from the gender identity they've been socialized with since birth. This was a topic we had discussed throughout the course. For example, when we read the first chapter of Stephanie Brill and Rachel Pepper's *The Transgender Child*, we talked about the following remark from a 7-year-old transgender boy:

It's so funny when people ask me how I know I am a boy. I just ask them, how do *you* know you're a boy? It's such a silly question. You just know those things. I've known all my life![1]

We also talked about Reiff Hill and Mays' discussion on defining gender:

You know all that boy/girl stuff you learned about growing up? The pink and blue, the dolls and trucks, the tutus and ties? That's how your culture defines gender. There are expectations about the way you should look (and the behaviors and interests you should have) if you have a particular kind of body ... Maybe your body is like other boys' bodies and you see yourself as a boy and you act in the world like other boys; well, that's your gender. There are tons of ways to be a girl or a boy, and tons of options in between and all around these. You don't have to choose. Your gender is where you feel the most comfortable, and it can grow and change just like the rest of you.[2]

However, for Teacher 1, reading about gender identity in a book was different from hearing Violet and her siblings William and AJ (pseudonyms) talk directly to her about it.

TEACHER 1: *Think about a moment in the videos that provoked an emotional response for you. What was it and why do you think that you responded emotionally to that moment?*

Viewing the interview about advice for teachers with the Addley kids was the first time that I witnessed young children speaking openly about issues surrounding gender and/or sexuality outside of my schooling and/or in my role as teacher. What struck me the most when watching the video was their sense of conviction when suggesting [teachers] "... just let them be themselves" (Addley Kids: Advice for Teachers, June 15, 2015). William and AJ's individual responses demonstrated a level of maturity and were so simple and direct.

This resonated with me because it seems, with age, things become a lot more complicated than they have to be. Our own personal bias evolves based on our experiences, which in turn influences our teaching and we may find ourselves at odds due to a variety of factors created by our different identities (personal, institutional and/or social). By listening to William and AJ's advice, it made me consider how allyship and action are indivisible. If you think one thing but are not following through on another thing, then you are not successfully supporting your students. We must work hard to remain accountable to ourselves and our students. (Assignment by Teacher 1, December 2016)

William and AJ's advice provoked Teacher 1 to think about how her own biases might get in the way of supporting transgender or gender diverse children to be themselves. William and AJ's advice also provoked Teacher 1 to consider how allyship and action go hand in hand. If a teacher can't follow through on their desire to support a child by acknowledging the gender they identify with, for example, or by using the pronoun they requested, then they can't really consider themselves an ally.

The relationship between allyship and action was a topic we had discussed in some depth throughout the course. The topic was originally raised by my graduate student, benjamin lee hicks, and we had several conversations about the kind of action teacher allyship might entail. We came to understand that simply proclaiming to be an ally was not the same as being recognized as an ally by the people we hoped to ally ourselves with. We also came to understand that allyship involved building trusting, accountable relationships with students and families.

The work of allyship was recently discussed by a group of panelists on the American podcast *Codeswitch,* hosted by the National Public Radio. *Codeswitch* features stories and discussions on race, ethnicity, gender, sexuality, and culture and how they play out in American people's lives.[3] In an episode called "Safety-Pin Solidarity: With Allies, Who Benefits?" (March 8, 2017), *Codeswitch* host Shereen Marisol Meraji and producer Karen Grisby Bates explored the intricacies and complexities of allyship with four activists: ShiShi Rose, who helped organize the Women's March on Washington on January 21, 2017, to advocate for human rights, women's rights, LGBTQ rights, immigration reform, healthcare reform, reproductive rights, environmental issues, racial equality, and freedom of religion; Taz Ahmed, co-host of the *GoodMuslimBadMuslim* podcast[4]; Reverend Timothy Murphy; and *Codeswitch* editor Juleyka Langtigua-Williams. To start off the panel discussion, Bates began with the question, "What does it mean to be an ally?" Here is what each of the panelists said:

SHISHI: I can go first. This is ShiShi speaking. I know that a lot of people look at the term of allyship and they think there's an end goal, but I think the bigger picture is that we're always learning. And so, for me, I feel like that's the biggest definition, is to step into it being willing to support other people and always with your thinking cap on.

KAREN: Anybody else?

TIMOTHY: Sure, this is Timothy. For me, the way I can see it is "ally" is more of an action that's more important than a posture of being seen as an ally. So, in some ways, a verb versus a noun, so in that way allying is using access or resources or privilege to back up or support communities that are experiencing oppression or exploitation in some way.

KAREN: Taz?

TAZ: Yeah, I've been struggling a lot with this word. I think for me allyship and solidarity are two words that are in controversy right now. I do think there's kind of a problem behind that. We need people to be emphatic not sympathetic, and I think allyship is all about the sympathy versus empathy, which is what we need.

JULEYKA: This is Juleyka and I think it's an oxymoron.

KAREN: Why?

JULEYKA: Because allyship implies a bunch of compromises on the part of the person who is receiving the allyship, which I don't think we should have to make. And there's an implied power dynamic that has to be preserved in order for the ally to perform the role of allyship.

KAREN: Our producer Walter [Ray Watson] brought up a point that I have to admit I don't agree with but I still wanted to pose to you panelists, which is this: does the dynamic of being an ally always involve White privilege or some kind of privilege, and what if both allies are people of colour?

SHISHI: Hi, this is ShiShi speaking. I would say that even if you're a person of colour, or any other marginalized person, there's always some form of privilege that somebody can hold in some form. I mean, you can exist in both ways, even if your oppression totally overpowers whatever privileges you may hold. You know, you can be a trans woman of colour, for instance, but be able-bodied, and, you know, be, exist in a first-world country and be English-speaking in this first-world country. So boxing people in and saying, "Oh, you can only be oppressed or you can only have privilege" is where people mess up because it's not just about one thing.

KAREN: Anybody else?

TIMOTHY: Okay, yes. This is Timothy. I really have to affirm what ShiShi said that so often we try to make binaries of absolute oppression or absolute privilege and it's way more complicated than that. Muslims may be allies with the Black community in terms of racialized mass incarceration but the Black community might be allies with Muslims when it comes to a Muslim registry or ban on refugees, for example. So, the dynamics and the relationships are really what matters versus it as an identity or an essential element of one's being as an ally. I don't think that's a helpful way of thinking of it.

JULEYKA: This is Juleyka, and I have to disagree strongly on that point because part of the assumption in allyship is that what is good for me is not good for you, when, in fact, anything that benefits me as a citizen, as a woman, as a woman of colour, ultimately benefits everyone. And so when we disaggregate that mutual universal benefit we get into the type of categorization that we see now with the proposed, supposed Muslim ban. Right? It can't be that we wait until a particular group is singled out for a particular type of oppression that then we gather around that group. It has to be that we are constantly in a state of affront against injustices and inequalities and things that any of us at any point could become victimized by.

In the *Codeswitch* panel discussion there are several important ideas that are relevant to our discussion about teacher allyship in this letter. First, hicks' idea of allyship as action is taken up by Timothy Murphy, who believes being an ally requires actively using access, resources, and privilege to support people and communities who are experiencing oppression. Second, teachers working as allies need to remember we can never be complacent about our work and what we know. As ShiShi Rose says, "There is no end goal in allyship, only ongoing learning." Finally, when thinking about how to build trusting, accountable relationships with LGBTQ students and families, I recall Taz Ahmed's comment that teachers need to understand the difference between sympathy and empathy. Sympathy involves feeling compassion, sorrow, or pity for another person's struggles. Empathy involves the ability to take the perspective of another person or recognize their perspective as their truth. Ms. Richards was seen as an ally by the

Addley family because she was able to act on Violet's understanding of herself as female. As Teacher 2 from our course writes below, Ms. Richards' empathetic support was important to the Addley family because it meant Violet didn't need to hide who she was at school.

TEACHER 2: *What are you taking away from the videos? How might this inform your future practice?*

> The story of Violet's teacher, Ms. Richards, was also quite powerful, in that she was in fact the one who encouraged Violet to put on her dress at school in the first place, obviously an experience that had a profound effect on both Violet and her family. As May stated, "It changed us!" (Addley Family: Transitioning at School, June 15, 2015). This teacher helped to ensure Violet was comfortable in how she chooses to express herself, not only at home, but in public, relieving her of any sense of having to hide who she was. (Assignment by Teacher 2 December 2016)

While Ms. Richards' allyship did have a profound effect on Violet and her family, allyship is complicated. Juleyka Langtigua-Williams calls allyship an oxymoron, an idea that is contradictory. While Ms. Richards brings action and empathy to her work with the Addley family, the reason she is able to act as an ally for Violet is because she has authority and privilege in her classroom: authority as an adult, and privilege as a cisgender woman. If Violet, as a transgender girl, had the same authority and privilege Ms. Richards had, she wouldn't need Ms. Richards' allyship. Put a little differently, if Violet went to a school where it didn't matter that her gender identity didn't match her sex assigned at birth, she wouldn't need an ally. To begin to create such a school, teachers need to provide their students with an opportunity to discuss what they know about gender identity and to question what they know.

This is a topic Karleen Pendleton Jiménez, a writer and professor at Trent University in Peterborough, Ontario, writes about in her latest book, *Tomboys and Other Gender Heroes*.[5] The book contains a wide variety of stories about gender gathered from approximately 600 children and youth in Ontario. Pendleton Jiménez, who identifies as Chicana and lesbian, collected the stories as part of a research study which asked students in Grades 4–12 to share what they knew about gender, gender transgression, and social responses to gender transgression. In her introduction to the book, Pendleton Jiménez writes this:

> I think gender, as a key component of human development (Benjamin, 1995), should be an important part of the school curriculum. Students shouldn't have to search for knowledge about gender diversity in the shadows or wait until they have left secondary school to find affirmation. Young people should not feel compelled to perform according to rigid notions of gender but should learn instead about their beauty and power of their instincts. I want them to become confident with their bodies and identities (p.4) ... Greater acceptance of gender diversity is possible through representation (Jennings, 2014) ... I write this book as a tactic to provide representation, to share at every opportunity what students say about gender and to provide a space for thoughtful discussion.[6]

By sharing stories like the one from a Grade 9 girl who loves "mudding on the four-wheeler and paintballing, but who also likes to dress nice with sparkles and dresses,"[7] and the one from a Grade 8 boy, whose 2-year-old cousin gets teased because "he likes to dress up like a princess,"[8] Pendleton Jiménez provides teachers with a broad range of possibilities for how children and youth might express their gender. The last chapter of her book includes lesson plans based on the gender workshops she conducted to collect gender stories from children and youth. Teachers can use these lesson plans to collect stories about gender stories from their own students. Pendleton Jiménez also shows teachers how to create lesson plans from the stories that have been discussed in the book.

While Teacher 2 discusses how important Ms. Richards' work was for the Addley family, not all teachers or principals are ready or willing to support transgender and gender diverse students in their schools. In the next letter, I'll share what our research team learned from another parent who did not have a "Ms. Richards" or a supportive principal to support her transgender child in school.

All the best,
Tara

Notes

1 See Brill and Pepper, 2008, p.1.
2 See Reiff Hill and Mays, 2013, p.3.
3 To listen to this podcast go to http://www.npr.org/sections/codeswitch/ and look for the episode called "Safety-Pin Solidarity: With Allies, Who Benefits?" (March 8, 2017).
4 See http://www.goodmuslimbadmuslim.com.
5 See Pendleton Jiménez, 2016.
6 See Pendleton Jiménez, 2016, p.5.
7 See Pendleton Jiménez, 2016, p.5.
8 See Pendleton Jiménez, 2016, p.28.

LETTER 11
LISTEN TO THE KIDS

Dear Teacher:

While the Addley family felt well-supported by Violet's principal and Ms. Richards, our interview with Dawn (a pseudonym) revealed that not all children who transition at school have as positive an experience as Violet had. Dawn has two daughters. Her older daughter was age 10 during our interview in 2016 and identifies as cisgender. Her younger daughter was age 8 and identifies as a transgender girl, just like Violet. Dawn doesn't live with the girls' father, and she and the girls' father share custody of their daughters. Dawn and her daughters identify as White.

When Dawn's younger daughter socially transitioned at the age of 8, she wanted to start fresh at a new school where people did not know that she had previously presented as male. While the health providers working with Dawn and her daughters also thought switching schools would be a good idea, the girls' father didn't want them to. So, the girls stayed at their old school and made the best of it, even though they weren't happy there. When I asked Dawn to tell us about her daughter's transition at school, this is what she said.

DAWN: ... It's been pretty difficult. Because it's been two years this month since she sort of started talking a little bit about feeling like a girl. And then it was in April 2015, where she chose out a different name, and has been pretty consistently identifying as a girl. So, [it] was really actually last school year, and part of the school year before where this was in play. And the school, like, I have to say wasn't super supportive at the beginning. I've talked to a lot of other parents in [my city], in [my school board] who had different experiences, but I think because the school had gotten a little caught up with the parents having a conflict, [they] weren't really thinking about the human rights of the child, and the safe school situation. So last year, not last school year, at the end of the school year before, I contacted the school and asked them if they would bring [a LGBTQ community program] to do education … they bring a trans-identified educator, like, into the school to educate the staff. And they bring books into the library, and they do different things to make the school a safe space, and then for an individual child, they can also make an accommodation plan for that child. So, I requested that, I didn't get much of an answer. I requested it again, and I eventually contacted the superintendent.

So, my understanding about that is that if a parent requests it then they have to do it, it's not really, like, a choice. But it took quite a bit of time, and I think that the school was a little bit like, "Mom is saying one thing, dad is saying something else, so we can't put accommodation in for the child." So then the program … said, "Well, we can come in and do the general education for the school, we're not gonna talk about which child is identified, even though we all know which child it is." So it [had] kind of got around that dad didn't agree [with his daughter's decision to transition]. So, they came in and they did the education last year, but still there weren't really a lot of changes in the actual school itself. They didn't make a universal washroom, which was something that I had requested. And then they also didn't allow her to use her preferred name. So sometimes she didn't write any name on her paper. And her teacher would write the name that she was given at birth in pen, last year. So, I feel, like, she didn't feel like school was a very safe place.

She told some of her friends, like "I'd like it if you use this name," but I think without the leadership of the staff, like it's a bit hard for kids to understand. Also, I'd say she was wearing, like, neutral-feminine clothes half the time and then, like, very stereotypically masculine clothes when she was coming from dad's house. So, that also was a confusing thing. Like, I think a lot of people really take their cue about gender from, like, [what] people are wearing, and, like, their haircut. And don't kinda get that the person doesn't necessarily identify differently just because their clothes have changed. It's like, if I put on a three-piece suit I wouldn't suddenly become a man. But people seem to see it that way without the education. So, last year was pretty difficult. And I think honestly a boy dressing in girls' clothes some of the time gets teased more than somebody who just identifies as a girl, even if they're, like, a trans girl. There's more difficulty in people understanding "Why is this boy wearing a pink shirt?" than there is in "Okay, this person has changed their name." And that's been my experience so far.

So, this school year has been better, because I think possibly the school may have gotten legal advice over the summer. And I think possibly they realized that I was going to file a human rights complaint, which I was. But I wanted to actually switch their schools. Like, I'm tired, I don't have the energy to be the one parenting and advocating. And we are the first family in this school kind of pushing it forward. Whereas the school across the street from my house they already have everything, and they already have one gender-fluid child who is actually friends with my child. So the school has everything in place already. So, to me, it's like, "Okay, let's just save the time, save the work, save the advocacy, save my child having to be the pioneer when they don't have a lot of confidence anyway, and just go to the school where everything is already there, they already have a universal washroom, the staff is already trained." So that would have been my preference, and both of my kids would have preferred that. Because my older one kinda feels like she has to look out for [her sister]. And then she gets asked a whole bunch of questions too.

But that [changing to the school across the street] didn't happen. So I kinda looked into what the actual rules were, and we made a meeting with the principal before school started. And then my daughter said, "I want you to call me by this name at school." And the principal was like, "What bathroom do you want to use?" And she was like, "I'm gonna use the girls' bathroom" and the principal was like, "What're you gonna do when the kids say . . ." And she said, "Well, I'm just going to say . . . and use the new name now." So then the school had no choice. Because when they hear it from the child directly, they can't say anymore that "it's a conflict between the parents," and "we can't make an accommodation without both parents on board" because of the human rights situation.

So, she started the school year with her new name. We had a case conference at the school, I think maybe about 10 days after school started. Because the kids see a psychologist in the community who has become a very good ally, and she didn't have a lot of knowledge about this area when we started seeing her, but, like, she has really done the work to educate herself, but also just to listen to the kids, which is, I think, what a lot of people don't do.

People sometimes get caught up in "I can't support this person because I don't know about this, or I don't know anything about trans people so I'm not going to help." But it's not really that complicated, it's actually really very simple. You just have to listen to somebody and then treat them with respect. It's not like you need a special education course. And I think that's just an excuse that people use not to be accountable, like "Oh I don't really have enough education in this area so I'm not going to do anything, because I might do something wrong."

But doing nothing is worse, in a way, than just, like, believing people. It's pretty, I dunno, to me it seems pretty straightforward. But my background is in social work, and I work at an organization that supports abused women, so the concept of listening and believing is already something that is part of my life, and it's more of a social justice organization. But, still, it's not like I got a manual in the mail that said "How're you going to raise your trans kid?" It was just like this happened, and I didn't raise this child in a gender-neutral way. Like they were pretty stereotypically dressed in boys' clothes and put into boys' things, like all the way along. It never even would have necessarily crossed my mind, though I wasn't 100 percent surprised, but nobody gives anyone a manual. So I think saying "I don't know about this" is not an excuse. You can educate yourself, it's not that hard.[1]

There is a lot to learn from Dawn's discussion of her daughter's experience of trying to transition at her school. Unlike Ms. Richards who was an ally to Violet, Dawn's daughter's teacher did not allow her to use her new name in the classroom. When Dawn's daughter chose to write no name on her assignments rather than write the name she had been given at birth, her teacher would write in her birth name in pen. This practice made Dawn's daughter feel unsafe.

While there was another school nearby that had already begun to do the work to support their gender diverse students, Dawn's daughters were not able to change schools because their father did not want them to. So, Dawn had to become an advocate for her daughter, and research how to launch a human rights complaint against the school her daughters were attending. Her younger daughter had no choice but to become a transgender pioneer in her school, even though Dawn believed she didn't always want to take on this role.

Fortunately, Dawn's family did find an ally in a psychologist they began working with. Although the psychologist didn't have a lot of knowledge about transgender children, she did the work to educate herself. And, she chose to listen to what Dawn's daughter had to tell her about how she wanted to live her life. The psychologist's allyship has shown Dawn that supporting transgender children is not very complicated. It's really very simple. Teachers just need to listen to what their students are telling them and then educate themselves on what they don't know, just like Dawn herself had to do. For a list of resources on gender, gender identity, and gender expression, see Letter 7, the "Resources" section, and "The Unicorn Glossary" at the end of the book.

When I contacted Dawn to ask her if she approved of the way I used her words in this letter, she gave me an update of how her family was doing. Since our interview together, Dawn has gained full custody of her children. Her daughters have switched schools, and the new school accepts her younger daughter as trans. She says it was a non-issue for the school. Dawn's younger daughter uses her preferred name and the girls' washroom at school. None of the other children knows she's trans. Overall, Dawn says, school is a much safer place now for both her daughters.

All the best,
Tara

Note

1 Interview, November 7, 2016.

LETTER 12
EASY TRANSITIONS

Dear Teacher:

In this letter I want to share the experiences of a family who worked through two gender transitions with teachers and principals at their suburban French Catholic elementary school. The first transition was parent Maxime Redecopp (formerly Beausoleil) in April 2016. Max (AFAB – assigned female at birth), who talked about the differences between tolerance, acceptance, and support in Letter 3, identifies as White, Francophone, and transgender. Below, Max describes his experience of transitioning as a parent at his children's elementary school. Max and his partner Ryan Redecopp have two children enrolled at the school. At the time their daughter was in Grade 1 and their son was in daycare.

MAX: And, so I approached them [the school], and I said, "This is the new reality of our family, and you're going to be hearing different names and different pronouns, different experiences than you may have heard previously. Going forward, this is our family. And if you need more information I am more than happy to meet" ... And I sent that to the principal, the vice-principal, [my daughter's] teachers, and the daycare that is also connected [to the school] because [my son] was going to the daycare as well ...

　　... They were so supportive, I was just taken back. I couldn't believe it. I got messages of support from all of the, all of the administration, just saying "This is fantastic, thank you for letting us know. We are going to be doing as much as we can." In fact, the next day, one of the women at the daycare – and it was like pre- and after-school care, so it was either before or after [school] – took all the children and brought them on the mat and started talking about families, and used different dolls, and things, and figures and said, "Show us your family." And when it finally got to [my son] at one point, you know, he was discussing "This is my papa, and this is my other papa," and then it was just, like, without a beat, the other kids were like, "Oh, you know, I have like, two aunts . . . And so it started a conversation and she [the teacher] had said that she had never seen children so happy to discuss their families. And it was a very, she even said that it was a safe space and they [the children] knew that they didn't have to worry about any judgement. And she, the kids were just like, "Oh that's, really, oh that's great!" and "What about you?" "Wow, really neat!" So, it was really interesting because it opened up a whole new dialogue, I guess, that they hadn't done before. But I felt that the way they approached it was just so top notch.[1]

Max was very satisfied with the way his son's daycare teacher opened up a conversation about families in her classroom. The teacher provided the children with a variety of dolls and figures and let them tell each other who was in their family. This gave Max and Ryan's son the opportunity to talk about his two papas, and another child to talk about their two aunts. The children were given a space to listen to each other talk about their families in ways that made sense to them.

The work Max and Ryan did with their children's school when Max transitioned in April 2016 ended up being very important the following summer when their daughter (AMAB –assigned male at birth) came out as a transgender. Here's how Max and Ryan talk about their daughter's transition at school.

MAX: I sent the school a message and I said, "And even more change in the family." And so they were just flabbergasted. I think the initial reaction by one of the women at the daycare centre was "Oh well" – you know, I think it's, you know, the typical rhetoric of like, you know, "Oh, kids don't really know, of course, they are going to question who they are." And I went, "I'm taking my daughter's lead," and left it at that.

But since [then] not a peep, not a problem. Everybody has just been so wonderful. It's been so wonderful. And, like Ryan said, when we walked into that meeting room to meet [my daughter's] teacher, the principal and the vice-principal, they were offering all sorts of different things ... I sent them a ton of documents and I said, "Whichever one you want to read, read. At least it will give you some basis of information." And they said, "Oh actually, we read this." It was a document which was basically a more recent one. There's so many documents that I just can't remember now ... There were post-it notes and notes, and supposedly ... they had really gone through it. And I went "Oh" ...

... We came to the table with, I had, I had their policies, and I had everything printed. So, I was just like, okay, I'm not guns a-blazin', but if I hear any, if it's going off the rails, I'm just going to have to bring these out.

RYAN: They wanted to make it work though.

MAX: They wanted to so much.

RYAN: They really wanted to be an example of the new society. They said themselves, even five years ago, had a family come to the table, they would have been a little bit more shell shocked. But now, you know, the new norm is I guess it's not the normal, which was expected previously. You know the new normal is just every family is different ...

MAX: That's true. I mean, every month –

RYAN: [Our daughter] gets to talk to the school counsellor ...

MAX: ... Which is fantastic. And she loves it. She's like, "I met Madame Suzanne [a pseudonym] today." And it's just really nice to know that, and we've said this to [our daughter], we've said, "Listen, there's someone at school available to you at school outside of your friends, your teachers, you know, the school principal and so on, that is safe for you to say whatever you need to say. And you don't have to worry about it getting back to us or back to anyone. So, just let it all out. Anything." And I think she's like, "Uh, okay." And so far, from the counsellor, I've just been hearing, like you know, "Yeah she's just a regular kid." I'm like, "Oh, okay, great." So, obviously you hear some very scary stories about, like, the mental health issues that come along with transition, or that are exacerbated by traumatic experiences when coming out and so on. And I was just very worried, we were both worried just making sure that her mental health state ...

RYAN: We are aware of the stats.[2]

MAX: Yeah, we are very aware ...

RYAN: ... [but] we've had every resource available at our fingertips, and we were very educated to begin with. So we didn't have a huge learning curve. We've been very, very fortunate and very privileged in that sense that this has been a very easy transition in the sense that, in the sense that everyone has been very, very well supported the entire way through.[3]

Unlike Dawn, Max and Ryan have been institutionally supported by their school. They are particularly pleased their daughter has regular access to a school counsellor, another adult who she can talk to, other than her parents. Max and Ryan know that children don't always tell their parents when something isn't going well at school because they don't want them to worry. Knowing that their daughter can talk to Madame Suzanne if she is experiencing any distress is very important to them.

Madame Suzanne is not only available to work with Max and Ryan's daughter. She is also available to work with the school's teachers and principals. As Ryan says, "She's also there to help the teachers learn and answer questions and provide, I guess, counselling for them if they are finding things new or difficult."[4] Max adds,

When it comes to the teachers, I just wanted to make sure that, you know, that there is yet another layer of support [because] they are the first line. So I said [to her], "Get them ready, make sure they are okay, [that] they have the terminology they need, the concepts, and the tools that they need." And then, you know, we'll work heavily on just making sure the lines of communication are open ...[5]

When Max and Ryan first started working with Madame Suzanne she didn't have a lot of knowledge about transgender children.

MAX: ... [W]hen I first spoke to her, she said, "It's something new, but it's something that I am super interested in, and I want to help." And

I went, "Wow, okay great." So, [she was] already open, and I went, "Perfect" ... And she said, "So if you have anything that you want me to read, or think that would help, that I could use to also impart on, you know, tools and resources for the teachers and so on." I was like, "Oh, are you sure you really want me to send you everything?" ... [a]nd she was like, "Yeah, yeah." I just kept sending her links ... all these amazing resources. And she was just like, "This is incredible." She was like, "There's a plethora of resources" ... [s]o I have full confidence that, regardless of her experience at that time, the fact that she was open to do that, I went "Okay great."

In Letter 11, Dawn suggests, teachers need to listen to what it is their transgender students are telling them and then educate themselves on what they don't know. This is exactly what Madame Suzanne, with support from Max and Ryan, has done. It is something that other teachers and counsellors can do too.

While Madame Suzanne, like Ms. Richards in Letter 9, provides us with an excellent example of teacher allyship and shows us the importance of having a staff member like Madame Suzanne available to answer questions (in the same way May Addley in Letter 9 answers questions at her daughter Violet's school), having an on-site counsellor is not the same kind of institutional response to a student's decision to transition at school as creating a school-wide curriculum which teaches *all* children there are many ways for them to express their gender (see a discussion about Karleen Pendleton Jiménez's work in Letter 10). A curriculum that gives children an opportunity to learn that there are many ways to be a girl or a boy and that some people don't identify as a girl or a boy at all, but as someone "in-between" (see a discussion on hicks' work in Letter 22), not only provides students with many more options for gender self-expression, it may also address the issue of gender-based harassment and bullying at school. I take up a discussion of harassment and bullying at school in Letters 19 and 20, and will return to this idea of the potential of gender inclusive curriculum to create safer and more supportive schools for LGBTQ students and families.

All the best,
Tara

Notes

1 Interview, November 6, 2016.
2 To provide an example of the kind of statistics that worry Max and Ryan, a recent survey of 268 transgender youth in Ontario between the ages of 14 and 25 found that nearly two-thirds reported self-harm in the past year; a similar number of both older (aged 19–25) and younger (aged 14–18) youth reported serious thoughts of suicide; and 43 percent of older youth had attempted suicide. The study is called *Being Safe, Being Me*, and is believed to be the first Canadian health survey to focus on transgender youth. See Saewyc et al. 2017 for further details.
3 Interview, November 6, 2016.
4 Interview, November 6, 2016.
5 Interview, November 6, 2016.

LETTER 13
THE HARM WE'VE DONE

Dear Teacher:

In this letter, I discuss the experiences of Two-Spirit youth and Two-Spirit families at school. The term "Two-Spirit" is used by some Indigenous people who identify as LGBTQ. Writer and teacher Chelsea Vowel explains that the term "Two-Spirit" was chosen to replace the term *berdache* during the 1990 inter-tribal Native American/First Nations Gay and Lesbian Conference in Winnipeg, Manitoba. Vowel is a Métis woman originally from the Plains Cree-speaking community of Lac Ste. Anne, Alberta. She currently lives in Montreal, Québec. Vowel says *berdache* was a term her parents and grandparents used to refer to Indigenous transgender people and Indigenous gay men. Because the word *berdache* didn't always have positive connotations, the term Two-Spirit was chosen to replace it. Vowel writes the term was deliberately chosen to be an umbrella term, a specifically "pan-Indian" concept that could encompass sexual, gender, and/or spiritual identity. While she thinks it's a useful term because it is very broad and incorporates Indigenous beliefs, Vowel also believes, like many other pan-Indian concepts, it can sometimes be overly broad. As well, because it is an English term, "Two-Spirit" is also informed by settler beliefs.[1]

I first learned about the experiences of Two-Spirit youth at school when Alec Butler joined our research team and agreed to be interviewed for the *LGBTQ Families Speak Out* project. Alec is a Toronto-based filmmaker, playwright, and Two-Spirit/trans/intersex activist who worked with transgender and queer youth for several years. Alec, who uses the pronoun they, is currently studying Aboriginal Studies and

Sexual Diversity Studies at the University of Toronto. Below, Alec discusses the school experiences of Two-Spirit youth who identify as transgender. The youth Alec is talking about worked with them Alec in a community performance project about homeless transgender youth. The project was called *Trans Cabaret*.

ALEC: I think pretty well they all had a horrible experience at school from what I could gather. Very bad experience in school. Bullying. Being, uh, perceived as stupid somehow. 'Cause some of them are very shy so they were pegged as slow learners, stuff like that.

Um, most of them had to leave home because of being trans. Some of them lived in other provinces in rural areas, so they didn't get treated very well. So, yeah, a lot of them left school before they graduated. Didn't finish school and wanted to go back to school. Definitely wanted to go back to school and get more education ... so they could get jobs, which is a situation a lot of trans people have. They get bullied in school, they leave school. They can't get good jobs because they don't have the training or the education ...

... Labelling them as slow and stuff like that, I thought that was, that was really disturbing to me when I heard that ... Because I had the same experience in school. I was considered slow ... 'cause I was quiet and shy and I knew I was different, you know, from a young age, so I really felt for them going through that ...

... [But] I had a good connection with an English teacher, who picked up right away that I wasn't stupid. Um, so I got really good marks in his class. Every time I wrote something for him, he'd be like, "Wow, so good, so good." And, um, he even talked about it in class, "This essay is really good," *(laughs)* and stuff like that, and, um, and then I had a conversation years later with somebody who said, "Were you considered slow in school?" "Yeah, I was." She said, "Yeah, it might have something to do with your First Nations background, because First Nations children when they're learning in school, they take a long time to answer because they're thinking about their answer. But if you go to a regular school, they want you to answer right away, right?" ... This is why I was considered slow, because I thought carefully about what my answer would be.[2]

There are several important issues Alec raised in their interview. The first is about the impact of transphobic bullying (see Letters 19 and 20 for further discussion of bullying at school). Transgender youth who are bullied often drop out of school. Without a high school and university education, they have difficulty finding a good job, and are often unemployed or underemployed.

The second issue is about the way some Indigenous youth are labelled "slow" by teachers. Alec offers two reasons why. Looking back on their own school experience, Alec says they were shy and quiet because they knew they were different from other kids in their class. Being quiet and not speaking out in class was seen as evidence that they were, using Alec's word, "slow." As well, when Alec took time to answer a teacher's question, because they were thinking carefully about the answer they wanted to share, the additional time they took was also seen as evidence they were "slow."

When I asked Alec what advice they had for teachers working with Two-Spirit transgender youth, this is what they said.

ALEC: Educate yourself. About colonialism, about the [Canadian] *Indian Act*, what it did to, uh, to the families of this country. Uh, be compassionate. Listen. Listen more. Don't assume and label kids if you think they're slow. They might just be thinking. *(Laughs)*. Thinkers. And try to incorporate Native knowledges into your curriculum. Like, I love what they're doing at school now, which is acknowledging that they're on First Nations land ... Oh wow, that's amazing. Yeah, that's a good start ...

... In one of my university classes I talked about re-hauling the education system. Yeah, it is based on the colonial mindset, Western mindset, which is different from Indigenous mindsets, so yeah, incorporating more of an Indigenous mindset into the curriculum, like getting outdoors more, getting on to the land, language, teaching the language. We're taught French but we're not taught Cree, we're not taught Ojibwe, we're not taught, yeah, Mohawk. We share ... three of the major language groups, and, um, yeah, that would be a good start to even teach the language for one hour a week. That would be good ... Then there's the whole – even the physical setup of the classroom is hard to learn in for Indigenous people, 'cause it's all rows. Right? And Indigenous people learn sitting in circles facing each other. Yeah. That's a major one even here at U of T. Trying to have a circle in a classroom is very hard . . .

. . . I think it's very important to acknowledge what – the harm we've done. And, um, try and do something about it. We're losing a whole generation of Native Two-Spirit kids, right, who still have to go through this system, and it's not helping them. I think it's set up that way, it's set up to make them fail, right? And, um, yeah, I'm hoping that will change in my lifetime. I mean, they've been talking about this for how many generations? Two or three generations? Fixing this? And it has to happen now. Don't put it off any longer. People are getting frustrated. Parents are getting in despair. Children are getting in despair. They're killing themselves. Suicide is a huge problem right now, and I want it to stop.[3]

Alec's advice to teachers to educate themselves about the history of the Indigenous people's relationships with White European settlers who came to Canada reflects the recent *Calls to Action* set out by the Truth and Reconciliation Commission of Canada.[4] The commission was asked to investigate and report on what happened to Indigenous children who had been placed in Canadian residential schools between 1831 and 1996.[5] Residential schools were government-sponsored religious schools established to assimilate Indigenous children into Christian Euro-Canadian culture. Many children were physically and sexually abused in these boarding schools, and the commission reports an estimated 3,200 children died from tuberculosis, malnutrition, and other diseases resulting from poor living conditions. The chair of the commission, Justice Murray Sinclair, has been quoted as saying this number is probably much higher because the burial records of the children who died were "very poor".[6]

The establishment of the Truth and Reconciliation Commission of Canada was a part of the 2007 Indian Residential Schools Settlement Agreement between the government of Canada and approximately 86,000 Indigenous people who were enrolled as children in the residential school system.[7] At the end of its report, the commission published 94 calls to action, which urge all levels of government in Canada (federal, provincial, territorial, and Aboriginal) to work together to change policies and programs in an effort to repair the harm caused by residential schools. The calls to action are divided into two parts: *Legacy* (calls 1 to 42) and *Reconciliation* (calls 43 to 94). The goal of these reconciliation calls is to renew relationships between Indigenous and non-Indigenous people so that they are based on mutual understanding and respect. As Alec argues, key to developing new relationships is the responsibility of learning about colonialism, learning about the *Indian Act* of 1876, which made it compulsory for Indigenous children and youth to attend residential schools, and understanding the impact the residential school system has had on Indigenous families.

In addition to interviewing youth worker Alec for the *LGBTQ Families Speak Out* project, we also interviewed three Two-Spirit families. The parents in two of the three families echo Alec's call for education and argue that Indigenous history and the legacy of residential schools need to be taught – accurately – in schools. For example, parent Catherine Hernandez told us a story about how her daughter had to "unlearn" some of the things she had been taught about Indigenous people at school. Deepening the discussion about the intersection of queerness and Indigeneity, Catherine argues such unlearning is an important part of being queer. While Catherine herself identifies as queer and Brown, her partner, Nazbah Tom, identifies as Two-Spirit, and Catherine considers their family an Indigenous household.

CATHERINE: . . . because we are an Indigenous household . . . we have to be constantly unlearning things and thankfully we have a kid who is perfectly fine with unlearning. She's grown up in a household where she knows when she comes home she's gonna be getting a completely different story . . . And that's part of being queer, you know, it's that queer is not just our sexuality, it's a constant questioning of where we are placed in society . . .

. . . I remember when [my daughter] was about, um, seven-ish, I think, her teacher said, when they were doing Aboriginal Studies, they said, um, "Indigenous folks live on reservations because the government put them where nature could thrive."

Who says that? I mean . . . [I] cannot believe that a teacher would believe that. That there's some sort of place with, like, rainbows and unicorns and, and, you know, pastures and clean water that they are imaging are happening on reservations.

So, of course, [my daughter] ... being a queer spawn ... [decided] "I would like to do a project that is the complete opposite of this." So, she made a project, presented it to the teacher, about residential schools and, like, that's what she wanted to focus on because she felt that other kids would connect to that particular subject matter when it comes to Indigenous history.

And the teacher refused to acknowledge it.

Thankfully, because of ... the daycare we go to [in a school where] ... there is a very high Indigenous population ... we went ... to the principal [there], and she put it up [in her school].

And [my daughter] was very proud of herself ... I'm just appalled that a teacher would believe that, that nature thrives on a reservation ... I'm just, like, I'm really concerned about, like, what kind of education this teacher received.[8]

Under the *Indian Act* of 1876 (discussed above) a reserve is land held by the Canadian government for the "use and benefit" of First Nations communities. Historically, reserves were created under treaties and other agreements between the government and First Nations communities.[9] While Catherine's daughter's teacher taught her students that reservations are places where nature can thrive, in reality living conditions on many reserves are substandard. For example, families living on some reserves don't have adequate housing or clean drinking water, and First Nation leaders have linked such poor living conditions to high suicide rates among Indigenous youth.[10] Earlier, Alec Butler also talked about how suicide is a huge problem for Indigenous youth. Like Alec, Catherine believes her daughter's teacher's lack of information and understanding about Indigenous history and current issues facing Indigenous people can be attributed to a lack of education. Parents Nicole Tanugay and Mita Hans agree. Nicole identifies as Two-Spirit and Mita identifies as Punjabi. When I asked Nicole and Mita what work teachers need to do to be able to develop and teach a curriculum that works towards reconciliation, this is what they said.

NICOLE: Having, um, First Nations come in and do education, going to pow-wows, going to Native events. The teachers should be doing that just to kind of know what they're talking about, instead of [our daughter] – how old was [she]? She sent me that video that I was just horrified at. They [her class] were doing some sort of a dance – like a circle dance, the round dance, and it was awful how it turned out because the teachers were just letting the kids do whatever, and they were being pretty, like, racist. Like kids were *(imitates a sound and gesture the kids have seen on television)* and doing the war dance thing and when [my daughter] showed it to me I told her, I said, "You know, that's not correct ..."

MITA: ... And this is where you hope that the teacher would have stepped in and said, "Well, actually this is how people do what they do and it's not appropriate for everybody to do what they do and sometimes it's really inappropriate when somebody who's not from that culture does that." Can we teach that?[11]

In answer to Mita's question, "Can we teach that?", the answer is yes. At the Ontario Institute of Studies in Education, our Master of Teaching program has recently begun to offer a curriculum and instruction course called Social Studies and Aboriginal Education. The course is designed for teacher candidates who will teach Grades 4–10. It provides an introduction to the teaching of Social Studies (Grades 4–6), and History and Geography (Grades 7–10) within the context of Indigenous understandings. A second course, which all teacher candidates in the program are required to take, is called Indigenous Experiences of Racism and Settler Colonialism in Canada: An Introduction. This course aims to help new teachers understand the experiences of Indigenous people in Canada through the lenses of racism and settler colonialism. The course acknowledges that Canadian schooling has a historical and contemporary role in reinforcing racism and maintaining settler colonialism, especially through the creation of residential schools, and it encourages teachers to become familiar with the consequences of this ongoing history so they can learn to develop new relationships between schools and Indigenous families and communities. Our hope at the Ontario Institute of Studies in Education is that these courses will inspire and support a new generation of teachers to begin to repair the harm caused by residential schools. As Alec Butler says, "It has to happen now."

All the best,
Tara

Notes

1 See Vowel, 2012.
2 Interview, June 7, 2017.
3 Interview, June 7, 2017.
4 See Truth and Reconciliation Commission of Canada, 2015.
5 Miller J. R. (2012) and Marshall, T. (2017) "Residential schools." *The Canadian Encyclopedia.* https://www.thecanadianencyclopedia.ca/en/article/residential-schools/.
6 Mas, S. (2015) "Truth and Reconciliation offers 94 'calls to action'." *CBC News*, December 14, 2015. http://www.cbc.ca/news/politics/truth-and-reconciliation-94-calls-to-action-1.3362258.
7 Marshall, T. (2013/2016) "Indian Residential Schools Settlement Agreement." *The Canadian Encyclopedia.* https://www.thecanadianencyclopedia.ca/en/article/indian-residential-schools-settlement-agreement/.
8 Interview, June 29, 2017.
9 McCue, H. (2011) and Parrott, Z. (2015) "Reserves." *The Canadian Encyclopedia.* https://www.thecanadianencyclopedia.ca/en/article/aboriginal-reserves/.
10 Fontaine, T. (2016) "Poverty, inequality fuelling suicide crisis, First Nations leader says," *CBC News*, March 13, 2016. http://www.cbc.ca/news/indigenous/poverty-inequality-fueling-suicide-crisis-1.3487028.
11 Interview, July 26, 2017.

LETTER 14
SEX EDUCATION

Dear Teacher:

In September 2015, the second year the research team was conducting interviews with LGBTQ parents, the Ontario Ministry of Education introduced an updated Health and Physical Education Curriculum that included new expectations around sex education.[1] The previous curriculum had not been updated for 15 years, and, while much of the new curriculum was the same as the previous one, the additions reflected a variety of changes that had taken place in society since the previous curriculum had been written. For example, the updated curriculum included discussions on cyber-bulling, sexting, and consent. It also included discussions on differences around gender identity and sexual orientation.

To illustrate, children in Grade 3 were expected to learn about people's visible and invisible differences and how to show respect for differences in other people. Gender identity and sexual orientation was included as an example of an invisible difference, along with things such as cultural values, beliefs, and family background. Several parent groups publicly opposed some of the additions, including the discussions on gender identity and sexual orientation. However, despite this small but vocal parental opposition, the 2015 curriculum was implemented and taught in schools.

In the fall of 2018, the newly elected Conservative government in Ontario repealed the 2015 Health and Physical Education curriculum for elementary students and replaced it with an interim curriculum which includes sex education material created 20 years ago in 1998. Below, Dawn, whose daughter socially transitioned at elementary school (see Letter 11), was concerned about the sex education information, examples, and "teacher prompts" (phrases to help teachers answer students' questions) included in the curriculum. She is afraid they might not be safe for transgender, gender diverse, and non-binary students. Although Dawn is referring here to the 2015 curriculum, her concerns apply to the interim curriculum her daughter's teachers must currently use.

DAWN: [There is] a really big gap in terms of sex ed for gender nonconforming folks, because before I knew that she [Dawn's daughter] identified this way, we had just the regular book about puberty and stuff that I had shown to my older daughter, and it was for 4–7-year-olds.

   And I would show it to my younger daughter, before I knew. And she would be really upset and would throw the book under the bed, and I didn't really know why. And I was worrying about all kinds of things, and then I clued in when she started identifying as a girl. I was like, "Oh, those books are really not safe, I'm such a bad parent, I've been totally traumatizing my child."

   So, we found another book, there's a book called *Sex is a Funny Word*, but even now I have a hard time getting the conversation started, because I think she was *so* traumatized by all these "the boys grow up to be men." So, there needs to be like, like, I think just having my experience, like, I talked to them one time and I'm, like, you know, "You have the sperm and the egg and they join together to make a baby." And my younger child was like "So, I have little tiny eggs inside of me, mommy?" And I was like, "Oh dear, this is going to be complicated." So, I think there needs to be, that needs to be considered in sex ed in schools. Because you're actually going to traumatize gender nonconforming people by teaching them about puberty and stuff in a way that doesn't include them, like, just based on my own experience with a very small child that's not even at that stage yet.

   So, I think that's something that teachers should be aware of too, like the way that you teach physical education and about puberty and stuff. Maybe that's better to come from an expert, rather than just a teacher that has no idea. Like, I can just imagine how many kids sat in that class and were just completely freaked out, and didn't feel like they were being represented. So I think that's important.[2]

Parent Evan Smith, who talks about being a queer parent and finding school support for children with special needs (see Letter 20), agrees with Dawn.

EVAN: ... [W]ith our daughter sort of getting to the age now where she's doing health class and stuff around sexuality and reproduction, all those pieces, I think that that curriculum really needs to reflect diverse families and especially trans and non-binary people and especially around, like, reproduction and body parts and puberty and all those things because I know from, like, the work I do in the community there's so many youth now who are coming out as non-binary and really sort of transgressing those gender norms. And our curriculum, I don't think is adequate at all to deal with that.[3]

To provide a context for Dawn and Evan's concerns, here is a list of curriculum expectations for students in Grades 4–6, which focus on puberty.

- In Grade 4, students learn about the physical changes that take place during puberty.
- In Grade 5, they learn about the parts of the reproductive system, menstruation, and spermatogenesis and how they relate to reproduction.
- In Grade 6, students learn about the effects of stereotypes, including things such as assumptions regarding gender roles, sexual orientation, gender expression, race, and mental health.

Students learn how to make decisions that show respect for themselves and others and help to build healthier relationships. If they ask about masturbation, the curriculum provides prompts for teachers to use in response.

While students learn not to make stereotypical assumptions around sexual orientation and gender expression in Grade 6, it is very possible the information they learn in Grades 4 and 5 about body parts, physical changes, and reproduction will reflect cisgender bodies and heterosexual relationships, not transgender bodies and queer or same-sex relationships. Both Dawn and Evan believe providing meaningful sex education for gender diverse students requires awareness and some expertise.

To begin thinking about what teaching a sex education curriculum that reflects transgender and gender diverse people might involve, I want to turn to the book Dawn mentioned, *Sex is a Funny Word*, by Cory Silverberg and Fiona Smyth. Written as a comic book for children age 8 to 10, *Sex is a Funny Word* welcomes the reader into its discussions about sex and gender by introducing us to four different characters: Zai (who has dark purple hair, dark purple skin, likes climbing on things, and dislikes mean people and bedtime); Cooper (who has red hair, glasses, orange skin, likes candy, math, swimming, and dislikes brothers, rain, and homework); Mimi (who has black and purple hair, blue skin, likes comics, gaming, skateboarding, and dislikes bossy people, spiders, and being wrong); and Omar (who has dark purple hair, lavender skin, uses crutches, likes reading, movies, long sentences, and dislikes big groups and yelling) (pp.4–5). Because each of the characters is different from the others and because each character has such specific likes and dislikes, there are many different ways readers can identify with one or several of the characters.

In the first chapter of the book, "Learning About Sex," a teacher whose name is Cory (like the author Cory Silverberg) tells his students that learning about sex is like visiting a carnival or a fair (pp.14–15): you can never do it all in one day, and it can be fun and strange and sometimes a little scary. Having given readers a heads up that they may find learning about sex is fun, but also strange or a little scary, Silverberg and Smyth provide us with a Table of Contents that includes topics such as "What is Sex?" "Learning About Bodies," "Boys, Girls, All of Us," "Touch," "Talking About Sex," and "Crushes, Love and Relationships."

The section called "Boys, Girls, All of Us" begins with Mimi saying, "I think this is the part where they tell us about the difference between boys and girls." Zai responds with "Only boys and girls? What about the rest of us?" In turn, Omar responds with "Excellent question, Zai. If everybody is different how could there be only two kinds of people?" Confused by where this conversation is going, Cooper says, "Wait, what?" (pp.72–73). Cooper's question gives readers a chance to pause and think about the idea that there are more than just two kinds of people (girls and boys).

As readers work their way through this chapter, they learn there are more than two kinds of bodies, but people call a baby a "boy" or a "girl" based on what they see. In a four-panel page called "What We Call Ourselves," a physical education teacher blows a whistle in panel one, and in panel two tells her students to line up: boys on the right, girls on the left. In panel three, Zai stands in the middle of the two lines, looking worried and confused. In panel four, the teacher asks, "What's the holdup, Zai?" (p.80).

Not having the words to explain what's wrong, Zai just says "Ummm . . ." On the next page, authors Silverberg and Smyth tell us, "When we are born, a doctor or midwife calls us boy or girl because of what we look like on the outside. They choose a word or label (usually boy or girl or male or female) to describe our bodies. But that's based on our outside, our cover, and who *they* think we are. What about our whole body, inside and out? What about who we think we are?" (p.81). Zai's worry about not knowing which line to join, the girls' line or the boys' line, and Silverberg and Smyth's question, "What about who we think we are?" provides an opportunity for children like Dawn's daughter to recognize themselves in the discussion about gender.

Earlier, Dawn talked about her daughter being upset when she read a book that told her boys grow up to be men. In *Sex is a Funny Word*, Silverberg and Smyth nuance that idea so there are other options for children such as Dawn's daughter:

> As we grow into being a kid and then an adult, we get to figure out who we are and what words fit best.
>
> Most boys grow up to be men, and most girls grow up to be women.
>
> But there are many ways to be a boy or a girl. And there are many ways to grow up and become an adult.
>
> For most of us, words like boy and girl, or man and woman, feel okay, and they fit. For some of us they don't.
>
> Maybe you're called a boy but you know you're a girl. You know how girls are treated and what they do. That's how you want to be treated and what you want to do.[4]
>
> Maybe you're called a girl but feel you're a boy. You know how boys are treated and what they do. That's how you want to be treated and what you want to do.

Maybe you aren't sure, or don't care that much. Maybe you don't feel like a boy or a girl. Maybe you feel like both. Maybe you just need some time to figure it out, without all the boy and girl stuff.

Because everyone's bodies are different, all our feelings are different too.

Part of being a kid is learning what you like, what you don't like, and who you are. That's part of being a grown-up too. We never stop learning or changing (pp.83–85).

Sex is a Funny Word is a resource that shows teachers how to work with the sex education curriculum in a way that reflects transgender and gender diverse children and youth. Like learning about sex, creating sex education for gender diverse students is like visiting a carnival: "You can never do it all in one day, and it can be fun and strange and sometimes a little scary." But it's important for teachers to begin thinking about ways lessons about body parts, physical changes, and reproduction can reflect LGBTQ bodies and experiences so that all children in their classes feel like they are being represented.

All the best,

Tara

Notes

1 Ontario Ministry of Education (2015). *The Ontario Curriculum: Grades 1–8 Health and Physical Education.* Toronto: Ontario Ministry of Education. Ontario Ministry of Education (2015). *The Ontario Curriculum: Grades 9–12 Health and Physical Education.* Toronto: Ontario Ministry of Education.

2 Interview, November 7, 2016.

3 Interview, June 19, 2017.

4 While copyediting the last draft of this book, *LGBTQ Families Speak Out* team member Kate Reid commented on the idea of wanting to be treated as a girl. "Just because I identify sometimes/mostly with being a female doesn't mean I always want to be treated how female people are treated, or always want to do what females do. This puts us back into the binary." Reid also commented on Silverberg and Smyth's use of the words "treated as a girl." In a sexist, patriarchal world, being treated as a girl sometimes/ often means being treated badly. Reid would have liked to have seen an acknowledgement of this in the book.

PART 3
LGBTQ FAMILIES AT SCHOOL

LETTER 15
MOTHER'S DAY AND FATHER'S DAY

Dear Teacher:

In this last section of this book I want to discuss some of the stories LGBTQ families have shared about their experiences at school. I begin with what families told us about Mother's Day and Father's Day. As mentioned in my "Getting Acquainted" letter, the families' thoughts and reflections have been documented in a set of video interviews that are available at www.lgbtqfamiliesspeakout.ca.

Celebrating Mother's Day and Father's Day is an important part of elementary school curriculum in Ontario. Several parents talked to us about what happened when teachers had their children make Mother's Day and Father's Day cards and presents. Shelby (a pseudonym), whose children have two moms, tells us the story below. Shelby and her partner both identify as White and lesbian.

SHELBY: And so, right from the get go, you know, our son had to deal with, "Well, I've got two moms." Right? But luckily Mother's Day is in May [by which time in the school year, her son's teachers know he has two mothers], so . . . the teachers said, "Okay, um, you can either make them both something for Mother's Day, or you can choose to do one now, and one for, say, Father's Day, so you're not left out when the other kids are doing something." And that's how they, right from the beginning, that's what pattern emerged. And every year it was kind of the same thing . . . [I]t worked up until Grade 5 . . . In Grade 6 he chose not to do something at Father's Day, and I also got a card on Mother's Day.[1]

Not wanting him to feel left out during Father's Day's activities, Shelby's son's teachers provided him with the option to make one of his mothers a Mother's Day card in May and his other mother a Father's Day card in June. While Shelby's son went along with this option until Grade 5, in Grade 6 it no longer felt right and he decided not to make any cards on Father's Day but instead to make two cards for Mother's Day. He wanted to celebrate Mother's Day with both his mothers.

Mary Evered (see Letter 5), whose daughter was also being raised by two mothers, told us a similar story. Mary and her partner also identify as White and lesbian.

MARY: I have a wonderful partner . . . and we've been together for 18 years. And, uh, we have a just-turned 12-year-old daughter . . . One of the very first things we always did was to meet the teacher on, you know, the curriculum night they have in September and say, "This is [our daughter's] family." And that, that our expectation was that her family would be treated, in any discussion of families, that we would be a part of it. And, and for the most part, I think that happened. But, you know, there was inevitably some discussion about, you know, how it all worked, and things like, "Oh, it's Father's Day coming up, let's make a Father's Day card!" . . . Her teachers were, were so wonderful when she was so young . . . They said, "Oh, it's Father's Day, oh well, here, make, make a card for your grand-dad." So they dealt with it that way. And they would give her extra time on Mother's Day to make two presents and two cards.[2]

Also worried Mary's daughter would feel left out on Father's Day, her teachers suggested she make a Father's Day card for her grandfather. However, they also made sure she had time to make two presents and two cards on Mother's Day. For Mary, the teachers' suggestions were very much appreciated.

MARY: I'm, I, I'm not really sure how much more we could have expected . . . She was the only child in that situation and they did take some very positive steps to make sure that she was included.[3]

For Michael Mancini and Ernst Hupel's daughters, Mother's Day was a bit more complicated. Michael and Ernst both identify as White and gay.

MICHAEL: Mother's Day and Fathers' Day was really interesting because, early on, the teachers would feel they were supporting us by having our children make Mothers' Day presents for us. But our daughters have birth mothers and they have a relationship with them.

ERNST: We are in touch with their birth mothers. So, early on [our oldest daughter] would go and say, "My teacher said I don't have a mom, but I do, her name is Heather." So, you know, the teachers were doing it to actually support us but after [our daughters] said "No, I actually have a mother" . . . they began to make Mothers' Day cards for their birth mothers and we send the cards to them and . . . [w]e get double Fathers' Day cards.

MICHAEL: It's a big day.

ERNST: It is! It's like Christmas here[4].

Here, a teacher's suggestion to make Mother's Day presents for two fathers didn't work for Michael and Ernst's daughters because they each had a birth mother. Instead, they chose to make Mother's Day cards for their mothers and make two Father's Day cards for their dads.

In all three of these stories, the children living in LGBTQ families eventually found a way to celebrate Mother's Day and Father's Day in ways that made sense to them. In two of the stories, the children had to explain to their teachers that they needed to do things differently than the other children in their class.

In the following commentary about Mother's Day and Father's Day, parents Jess Swance-Smith and Evan Smith (see Letter 20) talk about the importance of teachers not making assumptions about their students' families.

JESS: [Teachers shouldn't] assume what a child's family may look like . . . take their word for it. I mean if they say they have multiple people in their family, let them make those, you know, ten Mother's Day cards that they need to make. (*Evan and Jess laugh*). Or whatever, five

Father's Day cards because maybe there's, you know, ... maybe an aunt or an uncle who's like a father or a mother to them.

EVAN: I think one thing I really appreciate is that, for instance, at Mother's Day the school wasn't sure who identified, you know, as a mother, for sure, and so they just sent out, like, you know, a blanket message through our, you know, we have, like, an app we use to communicate with teachers and they sent out a message saying, you know, "We need to know who in your family identifies as a mother and should be getting a Mother's Day card."[5]

This last set of strategies seems particularly well-thought through as it allows students to make their own decisions about how they want to celebrate Mother's Day and Father's Day with their families.

All the best,
Tara

Notes

1 Interview, Nov 7, 2016.
2 Interview, Mar 11, 2015.
3 Interview, Mar 11, 2015.
4 Interview, Nov 5, 2016.
5 Interview, June 19, 2017.

Letter 16
Coming Out, Being Outed

Dear Teacher:

In a world that still assumes most people are heterosexual and cisgender, families who want teachers and principals to know they identify as LGBTQ have to tell them. While some families we interviewed believe disclosing their sexual and/or gender identity is helpful, others said they always think carefully about if, when, and how to come out at school. This careful thinking resonates with other current research that tells us young people living with LGBTQ parents make strategic decisions around when and how to talk about their family.[1]

Coming out marks both parents and children as different, and it's not always safe to be seen as different at school. However, Lara Atlas, a parent who identifies as lesbian and White, believes coming out at school is important. When asked what kind of advice she had for LGBTQ parents who were enrolling their children in public school, Lara said:

LARA: I think that they should just be very, very honest. Very genuine and authentic about their family and who they are. Because hiding who we are doesn't help anybody. And we're not going to move forward if we all remain closeted.[2]

The first time Lara came out as a lesbian parent was when she had to sign up her son for overnight camp.

LARA: When [my son Dale] was seven . . . we sent him to a week of overnight camp. And he was sort of interested in doing it, and it was just a week and it was for young, young kids and it was through the YMCA. And [we] signed him up, and [he was] good to go. And a couple months later, approaching August, I suddenly realized, you know, "We should let the camp director know." Because I suddenly realized Dale was going to be at camp, with a bunch of other kids from different places in Ontario . . . And I thought, "We'd better let the director know!" Like, it was something we hadn't had to worry about before, and it was something that suddenly occurred to me many, many weeks after signing him up. And it was one of those, I mean, I remember that today, because sometimes things hit you in such a way that you'll remember then forever. And I remember feeling a bit of fear. You know, not for him, but that we'd better connect with the camp director. There was no issue. And he had such a great time.[3]

While Lara felt a little fearful when she came out to the camp director (Would the camp director be supportive? And if the director wasn't supportive, would she and her partner still send her son to camp?), her disclosure didn't create an issue. Fortunately the teachers and principals at Lara's children's elementary school were also supportive, and perhaps it is on the basis of these positive experiences that Lara believes LGBTQ parents can and should come out at school.

However, despite this belief, Lara understands that coming out is something that has to be thought through with each new encounter and each new community. When her son Dale started high school, Lara noticed he was "negotiating things a little differently" than he had in elementary school. While Dale had been out as having two mums at elementary school, in high school he didn't bring it up. When we interviewed Dale himself about coming out in high school, this is what he said:

DALE: I usually find it very easy to talk about my family, but it's not something that I, uh, I talk about just without any social cues to need to explain it . . .

TARA: When you talk about social cues, what kinds of things do you have in mind?

DALE: Um, well, [if we're] talking about family at home, if they bring up a dad who isn't really, "I don't have a dad that I live with full time."

Or if there's something that I have to make more clear, or sometimes if there's people who are little bit, if they're homophobic, I bring up that I'm coming from an LGBTQ family.

TARA: And when you do that, more often than not does that go well, or are there moments where that's really difficult?

DALE: It usually, um, surprises kids who don't expect it to come from me, and I've never had much backlash from doing it because most of the time the community isn't very accepting of, like, bullying when it comes to homophobia or other topics.[4]

Although Dale hasn't experienced much backlash from coming out, he does think carefully about who he comes out to and who he doesn't come out to. He waits for social cues, such as finding out the person he's talking to (like him) doesn't have a father living at home. Sometimes, Dale makes the decision to come out when he hears a homophobic remark. He wants the person who made the remark to know he lives in a LGBTQ family and the remark is offensive.

While Dale has been able to make his own decisions about if, when, and how to come out at school, not all children are able to make the same decisions as Dale does. Some children are "outed" by their parents. For example, Karleen Pendleton Jiménez told us her butch appearance outed her children when she came to pick them up from school. Karleen is the lesbian, Chicana writer whose book *Tomboys and Other Gender Heroes* was discussed in Letter 10. While Karleen herself is comfortable with being out as a lesbian, she felt badly that her appearance took away her children's freedom to decide if, when, and how they wanted to be out at school.

KARLEEN: ... Looking the way I do, most people presume that I am lesbian. I mean, again, you could just not say it and have everybody whisper it. I don't know, I just can't, even, it's not my style. Um, I have to say, though, I did find it ... the hardest with the ... the older kids ... like I'm just out in every aspect of my life, okay? So, I did find it the hardest when I would go and pick the kids up, or take them to school. Because then people, the other kids, would start. They were just on it right away. "Oh, who's that?" "Oh well," you know, "Why does that person look like a boy?" You know, "How is that person related to your family?" And, so, um, I felt, like, just picking them up as a butch outed them. And I didn't, like that was probably the only place that I felt bad about it [being out] ... because I didn't want them – I wanted them to have the power to be out or not ... you know, to rest within them. And if they wanted to tell about their family, fine, and if they didn't, fine. But there was, if I was picking them up, there was no way to avoid it. And you could tell: the kids just start staring at you right away.[5]

What we learned from Karleen and some of the other parents we interviewed is that there can be consequences to being out or outed at school; consequences that range from having to answer questions such as "How is that person related to your family?" and "Why does that person look like a boy?" to being bullied at school. Children from LGBTQ families tell us some of the questions people ask don't feel hurtful. Others do. But, being bullied always hurts. It makes children and youth feel anxious, depressed, lonely, insecure, and angry. It also makes it difficult for them to concentrate in class. Some youth who are bullied drop out of school entirely, like the youth Alec Butler talks about in Letter 13. In Letter 18, parent Catherine Hernandez tells us what she did when she found out her daughter was being bullied for having a mom who was queer. But before moving on to Catherine's story of bullying, I want to share a story about a lesbian mother who chose not to come out at her daughter's school.

All the best,
Tara

Notes

1 See Epstein et al, 2013; McNeilly, 2012; Gustavson and Schmitt, 2011.
2 Interview, May 16, 2014.
3 Interview, May 16, 2014.
4 Interview, May 15, 2014.
5 Interview, February 3, 2015.

LETTER 17
NOT COMING OUT

Dear Teacher:

While most of the parents we interviewed came out as LGBTQ before their children were born, Victoria Mason (a pseudonym) came out when her daughter was aged 11. While Victoria's daughter has been supportive about her mother's new identity and life, she asked Victoria not to come out at her school. Below, Victoria tells us about her daughter's request. Victoria identifies as lesbian, cisgender, and Black.

VICTORIA: When [my daughter] was 11, her dad and I divorced. We had been separated for a good while, maybe almost two years at that point. Um, and so it was one of those things where I said one day, "You know I have something to tell you", and it was really kind of, she just took it, and she was, and at that point my mom did know, and it was really interesting because my daughter's response was overwhelmingly supportive. So much so to the point that I called my mom and my mom was like, "Well, you've raised her right." You know? And I can't remember exactly what my daughter said, but it was something like, you know, "This is, this is good mommy, we will get through it. If people are mean to you out in the world or whatever, we will get through this together. This is great that, you know, that you're kind of being honest about who you are." She actually even said, "So," she was trying to figure it out, "So you're like Lady Gaga." And I said, "Well, I don't really know about Lady Gaga ... " But, anyway, she was working with it, and she was good with it ...

... At my daughter's request I have not come out at school ... What they [the school] knew, what they've been through with us, because she's been at this school for five years, and had the same teacher. So, what they knew of us is that I was married to her dad when she started at the school, we went through a lot of challenges, and we ended up separating. Um, my daughter then was [living] part time with his, part time at his house, part time at my house. Some of the folks in school had journeyed that with us ... and the challenges of that, and [my daughter's] difficulties in dealing with that situation. So, during all that, after all that, then I came out.[1]

As mentioned in Letter 16, coming out marks parents and children as different. Victoria's daughter, who was known to the school as a child with divorced parents, did not want to be seen to be any more different than she already was. In addition to being marked as a child with divorced parents, Victoria's daughter was the only student of colour in her class. Here's what Victoria said about how being racially marked at school may have had something to do with her daughter's request that Victoria not come out:

I think another piece is that fact also that she is the only student of colour in her class ... So for her, how many ways, you know, maybe there's some of "How many ways do I not have to stand out here right now, when I am just trying to go to school and not have to deal with any of these other things?"[2]

When Victoria reviewed this letter to let me know if she approved of the ways I used her words, she asked me to add the following thoughts to her analysis. Victoria wrote that her daughter's fear of standing out was not simply a matter of not wanting to feel different from the other students in her class, it was a matter of being *marginalized* for being different. Having a lesbian mother was one more way for Victoria's daughter to be marginalized. In Victoria's words, "It was one more peg of identity that gave her less access to power and privilege in our world."

In an essay on Black lesbian mothers and daughters, written in 1995, Canadian writer Makeda Silvera also writes about the ways homophobia has challenged her daughters' response to having a lesbian mother.[3] She says,

> Being a Black lesbian parent is hard: this society holds that to be Black is to be undesirable, to be a woman is to be object, to be a lesbian is to be sick, and to be a Black lesbian mother is to be an undesirable object, one that is sick. Our children are not unaware of this, nor do they escape it."[4]

It's very painful to engage with Silvera's argument that Black lesbian mothers are seen as undesirable and sick. It was difficult for me to include it in this letter, and I know it is difficult to read. While we might think or hope things have changed since the publication of Silvera's essay in 1995, Victoria tells us that homophobia and racism, as well as stigma around divorce, still impact LGBTQ families. So, how might teachers and principals respond to the homophobia and racism that persists in society and schools? Victoria believes school staff need to "create a space where LGBTQ people and families are normalized."[5] Victoria says,

> And so that means that it's talked about. It's not that thing that we don't talk about ... it's part of the curriculum, it's part of the fabric of, of the school, just like the straight families are. You know what I mean? And so, yeah, I think, I think there has to be some intentionality ... [6]

Victoria realizes there is a contradiction between wanting the school to normalize LGBTQ families and not coming out to school staff herself. She shares,

> I struggle with that. So, here I am saying the school needs to be more out there, and here I am trying to be conscious and cognizant of how [my daughter] feels, and not feeling different.[7]

Coming out at school is fraught and complicated for LGBTQ families. Teachers and principals who want to create schools where it's safe for LGBTQ families to come out have to intentionally create a school culture where their families are expected, welcomed, and talked about. In Letter 22, I talk about what such a school culture might look like.

While it is important to write and read about the difficulties facing LGBTQ families at school so that we can work to create change, it is also important to talk about the pleasures and triumphs of LGBTQ family life. So, I want to end this letter with some more writing from Makeda Silvera, which talks about the happiness of lesbian mothering and partnering, and the comfort and the power of building queer community. Silvera writes:

> Still I feel tremendous freedom and joy in being a lesbian parent, in being a Black lesbian mother and in having a partner to raise my children with. It's often not tangible enough to explain – it is like having best friend, lover, sister, and more, all wrapped up in one package.[8]
>
> Determined to create a place for ourselves, an extended family, a Black, of colour, lesbian and gay community, we moved from our apartment to a house, armed with a vision of organizing Black and lesbians of colour who wanted, needed, an extended family. Our house was a bright array of colours: Black, Caribbean, Asian, Native lesbian mothers with children, living together, creating for ourselves what we were being denied. That "house" became a refuge for women of colour coming out, and the launching pad for a joyous and militant lesbian sexuality. We supported, comforted, laughed, and teased each other, strengthened by our new, if tiny, community. We had strong role models for our daughters and for many of the other children in the household. Our house was organized and full of love and hope.[9]

The strength and hope created in Silvera's house reminds me of the strength and hope in the GSAs Lee Iskander and other youth activists (see Letter 5) built in their schools. Like Silvera's house, GSAs can be a refuge for children and youth who identify as LGBTQ or live in LGBTQ families, communities where they can find friendship, support, and comfort.

All the best,
Tara

Notes

1 Interview, February 2, 2015.
2 Interview, February 2, 2015.
3 See Silvera, 1995.
4 See Silvera, 1995, p.314.
5 Interview, February 2, 2015.
6 Interview, February 2, 2015.
7 Interview, February 2, 2015.
8 See Silvera, 1995, p.315.
9 See Silvera, 1995, p.317.

LETTER 18
BULLYING: THE SCHOOL'S RESPONSIBILITIES

Dear Teacher:

Dealing with bullying is the responsibility of teachers and principals. However, when the principal of her daughter's school didn't come up with a suitable plan to address the bullying her daughter was experiencing, parent Catherine Hernandez came up with her own plan. Readers first met Catherine in Letter 13, where she shared her thoughts about needing to educate teachers about Indigenous history. In this letter, Catherine discusses the expectations she had of her daughter's school around bullying and how the school did not meet these expectations.

CATHERINE HERNANDEZ: I went to the principal ... and [told her what] was going on and that [my daughter was] a little scared to be able to come forward and to express her situation that she's being bullied at school for having a mom that was queer ...

I said, "She's a little scared ... She's a little bit worried about coming forward, so I'm coming forward to you on her behalf so could we have a meeting."

Now, instead of having a meeting with me, she goes behind my back, takes [my daughter] out of class and sits her down in her office as though she's in trouble, and says, "Your mom said this, this, and this, so I need to know all the details now," as if she's in trouble. And [my daughter] of course, she's just a little kid, she just froze and she says, "I don't think my mom knows what she's talking about. That's not true."

So, the principal calls me and says, "So, she said that nothing happened, that you didn't know what you were talking about." And so, when I talked to [my daughter] again, she, of course, said, "It's just 'cause I'm scared."

So, I went back to the principal and I said, "This is the reason why." I said, "Please can we have a conversation first before talking to my daughter?" And she said, "Well, I deal with things the way I deal with things, I've been doing this for many years."

I [shared] my concerns to a friend of mine who deals with, um, equity [issues] in schools . . . for the [school board]. [He] goes in – as long as the principal allows it – to do, um, inclusive workshops for both the staff and the students, which is really great if it's free. It just means the principal has to approve it because there's time being spent on it, but I think it's fantastic.

[My daughter's principal] said, "I don't need that, I've been doing this for years and the workshops that we have in the school are to be inclusive for everybody. I don't feel that we need to do anything about LGBTQ training." Even though [my daughter was being bullied].

It was so frustrating, and at that point I just gave up. I was like, "I don't have it in me, my daughter doesn't have it in her."

But then [my daughter's teacher] happened to ask me, "So, I heard that you're a writer, would you be interested in doing a workshop?" and I said "Sure." So I go in, I do a writing – not a writing workshop but a theatre workshop – so we learned some staging, I taught them some songs – blah, blah, blah. So, it's two days of workshop. At that time I also owned a home daycare, so you can imagine, I was doing [both these things] at the same time, having these very small children including a baby on my back. It was intense but we got through the workshop, the kids really loved it.

Then at the very, very end, uh, when we were doing our checkout, I said, "So, I hear that some of you have been making fun of my daughter," because I was, like, how else am I going to get to these kids? If the principal doesn't want me to speak to these kids directly, like, you know, what am I gonna do? What am I gonna do? How am I gonna get rid of this problem other than just speaking to them directly? And they had just gotten to know me. They liked my, they liked my theatre workshop … they already got to know me, they liked me … We had a relationship and that's exactly what I said, like, "I need you to respect my family."

I was very clear, all of them had red faces. [My daughter] was a little embarrassed but I didn't care … They just all had red faces and I said, "I want you to understand that what you are doing is actually unconstitutional. It's illegal, and I need it to stop." And the teacher had a red face, they all had red faces, and I was, like, "Thank you very much everybody, okay," [and] grabbed up all my daycare kids and left. It never happened again.[1]

When Catherine first found out her daughter was being bullied, she immediately went to the principal and asked to discuss the homophobic bullying her daughter was experiencing. This is exactly what educators who have expertise and experience around dealing with bullying in school tell parents to do. For example, in a blog entitled "Bullying Resources for Parents and Families," GLSEN (see Letter 2) says this:

> Children and youth often need help to stop bullying. Parents should never be afraid to call the school to report that their child is being bullied and ask for help to stop the bullying. Students should not have to tolerate bullying at school any more than adults would tolerate similar treatment at work.[2]

GLSEN also tells parents that most school boards and schools have anti-bullying policies in place that will help resolve the problem.

The principal at Catherine's daughter's school decided to deal with Catherine's report of bullying by talking to her daughter about what was happening. While such fact gathering is a necessary first step, when Catherine's daughter was called down to the principal's office she thought she was in trouble, and denied the bullying was taking place. Catherine asked the principal if they could talk about the bullying without her daughter present. The principal refused, and there was no further investigation of the bullying.

GLSEN tells parents that they should expect school staff to investigate concerns about bullying immediately, inform parents how serious it is, and what they plan to do about it. Because there was no further investigation of the bullying, no plan about dealing with the bullying was created. So, Catherine came up with her own plan. She found out her school board offered free professional development workshops for teachers and principals on how to respond to homophobia and asked the principal to arrange for such a workshop at her daughter's school. The principal refused, arguing the school didn't need any anti-homophobia training. After that, Catherine "gave up." Fighting to get a plan in place took up too much energy.

But then, because Catherine is a well-known writer and theatre artist, her daughter's teacher asked her to come and do a two-day theatre workshop with the class. Catherine used the opportunity to deal with the bullying on her own. At the end of a successful two-day workshop, Catherine told the students that she had heard some of them were making fun of her daughter. She then told them to stop and that they needed to respect her family. She also told them school bullying was against the law. It wasn't an easy moment. Catherine's daughter was embarrassed, her classmates were embarrassed, and the teacher was embarrassed. But, Catherine's plan worked. The bullying stopped.

While Catherine was able to make the bullying stop at her daughter's school, the responsibility to do so wasn't hers. It was the school's. GLSEN tells parents that school staff should meet with the children who are taking part in the bullying, tell them bullying is against school rules, and will not be tolerated. They also suggest, if appropriate, the school should administer consequences (such as a loss of recess privileges) to the children who bully and notify their parents. Finally, GLSEN warns teachers they should be careful to never blame the child who is being bullied. It is not their fault, and they shouldn't be made to feel responsible.[3] While GLSEN doesn't discuss how to talk with children and youth who are responsible for bullying, besides telling them bullying is against school rules, Nazbah Tom, Catherine's partner, had some very interesting ideas about working with bullies. I share their thoughts in the next letter.

All the best,
Tara

Notes

1 Interview, June 29, 2017.
2 https://www.glsen.org/bullying-resources-parents-and-families.
3 https://www.glsen.org/bullying-resources-parents-and-families.

LETTER 19
WORKING WITH BULLIES

Dear Teacher:

In this letter I discuss the ideas parent Nazbah Tom shared with us about working with bullies. Recall that Nazbah is Catherine Hernandez's partner, identifies as Two-Spirit, and uses the pronoun "they". The reflection they shared with us comes from their own experience of being a bully and was provoked by Catherine's story of her daughter's experience with bullying at school in Letter 18.

NAZBAH: ... [G]rowing up as someone who actually was a bully in school, like, I was a bully in grade school. Um, you know, I bullied actually another girl, um, and I called her a lesbian, because I was queer, right, and I didn't know to put the two together. But what did make sense later on was, you know, my dad was very violent in the household so, of course, I came out bullying other people, that was just what I learned to do.

Um, but what the principal actually ended up doing, which was not a way to also handle it, was they brought me in, they brought the mom and the kid in, and they basically were like, "You either apologize here and quit this, or we bring your dad in." And they didn't know my dad. Like, they didn't know how violent he is – he was. So in my mind I'm like, "Oh, you're threatening me with a bigger bully, so I'm definitely stopping." Right? So then I totally went into, like, a shell and I just quit contact with a lot of kids 'cause I'm like, "Oh, whatever contact I make, um, it's gonna be hurtful," 'cause that's what I know how to do, right, that's what I was conditioned to do.

Um, and what I wish had happened was that they would have brought us in, you know, in different ways. Definitely given me the message that, you know, "You're a good person but this behaviour needs to stop. And all of us together are gonna support you and then anyone else who's doing this." Right?

And then, also what's happening at home, right? Um, if there's stuff happening at home, "How can we support your parents?" Right? Because one of my older siblings ended up going into foster care because my dad hit her. So, there was intervention on that level. And you know, I'm actually against state intervention because they bust up a lot of homes anyway, most particularly people of colour homes.

If you have enough money you can buy your way out of jail, you can buy your way out of public service, right? . . . You can get yourself a private therapist and keep it hidden if you have enough money. But if you don't, then you're in the system and you're shit out of luck. That's sort of your life from then on . . . and you're shamed for it. All sorts of different things [happen then], right? And, of course, there's [the] reification of "Native parents can't take care of their kids, so White families should take them" . . .

. . . Um, so anyway, I wish they would've sort of, you know, done a lot of checks and balances and basically given me the message that I am okay, [my] behaviour's not okay, "Let's get you to learn something else." And then also, "Let's let the adults take care of it, this is not your job," right? And then [look at] what are we doing as adults to allow this to happen, right? Because I was getting lots of permission, indirectly, from everywhere that it was okay to do this.[1]

One of the important insights Nazbah shares here is that it is important to separate a bully's behaviour from who they are as a person. A child who bullies needs to be told they are a good person but that their behaviour needs to change. Bullies need to learn how to relate to people in new ways, and it's the job of teachers and principals to teach them new skills.

Educator Barbara Coloroso, who has been writing and teaching about school bullying for many years, agrees. In her book *The Bully, The Bullied, and the Not-So-Innocent Bystander* (annotated in the "Resources" section), Coloroso writes that children who bully need an opportunity to change their thinking and behaviour:

In disciplining a child who has bullied someone, we are concerned not only with mere compliance ("Don't bully. Say you're sorry and then just leave him alone"), but with inviting him [sic] to delve deeply into himself [sic] and reach beyond what is required or expected.[2]

For Coloroso, discipling children is different from punishing them. While punishment is something that is *done* to children, intervening with discipline can provide children with the tools they need to begin addressing the harm they have done. Coloroso offers a model of discipline that involves four steps:

(1) Show children who bully what they have done is wrong;
(2) Give them ownership of the problem;
(3) Give them a process for solving the problem they have created: how to fix what they have done (restitution), how to keep it from happening again (resolution), and how to heal with the person they have harmed (reconciliation); and
(4) Leave their dignity intact by making sure they understand that, while their behaviour was hurtful and unacceptable, they are not a bad person and they are capable of responsible and caring behaviour.[3]

Coloroso believes that discipline (in contrast to punishment or compliance) is a constructive and compassionate response to bullying. It takes into account the intent of the bullying, the severity of the behaviour, and the restorative steps needed to support bullies in changing their behaviour.

While I believe Coloroso's model of discipline based on the ideas of restitution, resolution, and reconciliation has a lot to offer parents, teachers, and principals, I have recently been introduced to the work of a group of researchers from the United Kingdom and the United States which has added to my thinking around school bullying. In April 2018, I attended a session on gender, sexuality, and bullying at the annual American Education Research Association (AERA) conference in New York City. The panelists in the session put forward an idea that complicates Barbara Coloroso's ideas about how to address bullying. Educational researchers Jessica Ringrose and Emma Renold are from the United Kingdom, and Elizabeth Payne and Melissa Smith are from the United States. All four researchers argue that addressing school bullying requires more than providing support to individual students who are bullied and those who bully. They say individualizing bullying behaviour neglects the role school and community culture plays in creating the conditions for bullying to take place. While most anti-bullying policies and educators frame bullying as anti-social behaviour, Ringrose, Renold, Payne, and Smith understand bullying as *prosocial* behaviour. They argue that bullying is a way for children and youth to police binary gender and heteronormative expression.[4] In other words, bullying serves as a way to ensure that boys act like boys, girls act like girls, and that everyone is engaged in heterosexual relationships. Children and youth who don't demonstrate traditional gender behaviour – for example, girls who prefer soccer over dolls and boys who prefer dolls over soccer – are frequent targets for bullying and harassment (a situation Karleen Pendleton Jiménez explores in her animated film *Tomboy*, which I spoke about in Letter 7 and is annotated in the "Resources" section).

Gender policing works to enforce cultural expectations for "normal" masculine/feminine expression. The further children and youth deviate from idealized forms of masculinity and femininity, the more vulnerable they are to bullying and other forms of violence at school. LGBTQ youth are often the most vulnerable.[5] Like Pendleton Jiménez in Letter 10, Ringrose, Renold, Payne, and Smith believe schools need to open up discussion about gender and gender policing and find ways to help children and youth learn that there are many different ways for them to express their gender. Without the opportunity for new learning, anti-bullying policies and practices will not make schools safer for LGBTQ students and families in any substantial, sustained way.

In sharing Ringrose, Renold, Payne, and Smith's ideas about bullying as gender policing, I don't want to dismiss Barbara Coloroso's model of restitution, resolution, and reconciliation. Returning to the Triangle Model I introduced in my "Getting Acquainted" letter, bullying needs to be addressed in several different ways.

First, bullying needs to be addressed at the level of ideas: children and youth need to learn there are many ways to express gender. Next, bullying needs to be addressed at the level of individual actions and

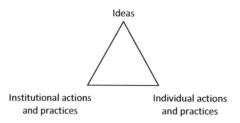

The Triangle Model

practices: teachers and principals need to intervene in incidents of bully-ing, and bullies need to make restitution. Finally, bullying needs to be addressed at the level of institutional actions and practices: bullying needs to be understood as a way of policing gender, and schools need to open up discussions about gender policing and work hard to challenge it.

Before ending this letter on bullying and policing, I want to return to Nazbah's reflection on their experience of being a bully. Right after Nazbah talks about how important it is for children who bully to be supported in the ways Coloroso writes about, they also tell us it's important for teachers and principals to ask questions about what's happening at home and find ways to support parents who bully. Asking questions about students' family lives, however, can be complicated and challenging. If the school finds out a child is being bullied or abused at home they are legally obligated to inform Child Services, who might decide it's safer for the child to be removed from their family and sent into foster care. This is what happened to one of Nazbah's older siblings. But, this is not the outcome Nazbah is looking for. What they are looking for is counselling support for parents that doesn't involve removing their children from their home.

Nazbah points out that families who can afford to pay lawyers and private therapists get the support they need to change their behaviour and keep their families intact. Families who cannot afford to pay for such support are at risk of not being able to keep their children at home. And, when Indigenous children are removed from their parents' home, it reifies and reinforces the mistaken and racist idea that Indigenous parents can't take care of their children. I respond to Nazbah's call for support for parents who bully in the next letter, in which Two-Spirit parent Evan Smith tells a different story about what happens when teachers and principals hold mistaken ideas about parents.

All the best,

Tara

Notes

1 Interview, June 29, 2017.
2 See Coloroso, 2015, p.197.
3 See Coloroso, 2015, p.198.
4 See Ringrose and Renold, 2010; Payne and Smith, 2012.
5 See Payne and Smith, 2013.

LETTER 20
QUEER PARENTS, AUTISM, AND LEARNING DISABILITIES

Dear Teacher:

In this letter, I discuss what Two-Spirit parents Evan Smith and Jess Swance-Smith have to say about their experiences of looking for cultural and learning support for their children at school. Evan and Jess's daughter goes to First Nations School in Toronto, while their son goes to a neighbourhood (non-Indigenous) school.

First Nations School is a public school that teaches the official Ontario curriculum at the same time as it teaches Indigenous knowledge, values, spirituality, culture, and the Ojibwe language. The school serves students from Junior Kindergarten to Grade 9. While many of the students at First Nations School are of Anishinaabe ancestry, the school welcomes children of all backgrounds. When I asked Evan and Jess whether the curriculum at First Nations School was serving their family well, below is what Evan said. Evan identifies as queer, trans, genderqueer, and Two-Spirit, and uses "any pronoun." I've chosen to use the pronoun "they" when referring to Evan in this letter.

EVAN: I think that at First Nations School things are so different, because, I mean, because we have a cultural understanding of Two-Spirit people as healers and often the elders in our community, and I think that that's reflected in the curriculum. There's lots of Two-Spirit people who work at the school who are very open about that. Um, there's always talk about, like, Pride Week, and there's definitely, like, diverse, you know, books in the library.

I remember when we first took the kids there, I emailed just to be like, "Just so you know, we have lots of queer and trans people in our, like, family and community, what's that gonna look like?" and the response back was almost like, "It's such a non-issue, like we can't imagine it being an issue and we uphold all identities in our curriculum." And I think often, yeah, there's Two-Spirit people who come in from the community who lead different workshops and cultural workshops, and so I think that it's just accepted.[1]

First Nations School is able to accept Evan and Jess's Two-Spirit family because it has a cultural understanding of Two-Spirit people as healers and elders, and staff who identify as Two-Spirit. The school also invites Two-Spirit members of the community to do cultural workshops with its teachers and students. When Evan and Jess's son was ready to start school, Evan enrolled him in First Nations School, just like his sister. However, because their son lives with autism, they needed to transfer him to a neighbourhood non-Indigenous school.[2] First Nations School didn't have the resources to support Evan's son in the way the neighbourhood school could. Using Kimberlé Crenshaw's idea of intersectionality, introduced in Letter 2, First Nations School didn't have the resources to support Evan's son's intersectional needs as an Indigenous child and as a child living with autism.

EVAN: Yeah, I mean in JK [Junior Kindergarten] he was at First Nations School and, I mean they pulled as much of their support and resources as they could but it just, it wasn't working out. He got transferred to a KIP Program, which is the Kindergarten Intervention Program for SK [Senior Kindergarten]. It wasn't suitable, because, I mean, it's for behavioral problems and so they didn't really understand, um, the autism piece and that his behaviour was triggered by sensory things, and processing stuff, and so that wasn't a good fit. Um, we – I pulled him out of the school, kept him home for a while, eventually put him into our neighbourhood school, because there were no spec. ed. [special education] classes at the kindergarten level available. So, we were just being told everywhere to "Wait 'til Grade 1, wait 'til Grade 1," and then got into an autism program in Grade 1, and, I mean, it's just been a world of difference.[3]

Autism spectrum disorder refers to a range of conditions characterized by challenges with social skills, repetitive behaviours,
speech and nonverbal communication, as well as by unique
strengths and differences. There are many types of autism which
are caused by different combinations of genetic and environmental
influences. The term *spectrum* reflects the wide variation in challenges and strengths possessed by each person with autism.[4] Fortunately, in addition to the program at the neighbourhood school
being a good fit for their son, Evan and Jess also feel the school
has accepted them as a queer, poly family of three parents (see
Letter 21 for a discussion on the experiences of poly families in
school). Below, Jess tells us about how their family has been
received by the school. Jess identifies as queer and Two-Spirit,
and uses the pronoun "she."

JESS: Well, I'm still fairly new to, well, I guess fairly new, to the family.
Um, I've been living with the whole gang for just over a year now.
So, I've been involved with school stuff. I'm on the list for parent
guardians. So, um, I felt, I've been, our family has been received
really well. Especially at [Evan's], [Evan's son's] school. Um, I think
they realize, um, because of maybe his autism, that three parents are
sometimes better than two.[5]

EVAN: Yeah, I mean his school's been really good. Like, we both got
Mother's Day cards from the school. They've been really accepting. I think in First Nations School we've never had a problem.
Um, I think it's because Two-Spirit people are held up so
highly in the school, and there's lots of Two-Spirit people who
work at school and I think, I mean, as Indigenous people we
have such a different way of understanding what family is and
have always. I think all of our cultures have always had extended
family raising children, so it's not weird to have sort of larger,
mixed, or blended families.[6]

The school's acceptance of Jess as a third parent to Evan's son, and its
ability to provide appropriate programming for Evan's son, is not
something Evan and Jess take for granted. When Evan was raising
their oldest daughter, who was 21-years-old at the time of the interview, Evan recounted experiencing a lot of conflict with the school.

EVAN: ... [When] my oldest daughter was growing up and, uh, I was with her mom at the time, we ran into nothing but problems, I mean, so, this is sort of, you know, like 1999 and onward. I, and, you know, they wouldn't let my partner sign any forms, they were always referring to me as the biological mother. Um, and I, I feel like that continued through her entire schooling experience, and, um, and with her schooling we always had to fight, we were trying to fight to get learning disability assessments and stuff done and it was always that we were terrible parents, and I wonder how much of that had to do with, well, we were young, we were both teen moms, but also that we were lesbian moms. And back then, I mean, we didn't really know other queer people with kids, or very few, so it wasn't so much the norm as it is now, in many ways, and, yeah, so we weren't able to access services for her. I mean, she dropped out by Grade 8, um, um, because of any lack of support, and I think that a lot of that had to do with our sexuality.[7]

Evan attributes the conflicts their family had with the school in the early 2000s to the school's deficit ideas about lesbian teen moms. While Evan and their partner fought to get their daughter assessed for a learning disability, they weren't able to get the services they needed and their daughter dropped out of school in Grade 8. The school support that is available for Evan's son in 2017 wasn't available to their daughter in the early 2000s. When I asked Evan what the school could have done differently so their daughter wouldn't have dropped out, this is what they said.

EVAN: I think that if we had been able to get adequate services, I mean, the difference between the services that she received or that we were fighting for her to receive versus what our son receives were night and day. Um, I think, you know, it was just always chalked up to our parenting, even though I mean we were always able to clearly lay out all of these other issues that were going on and it just, it always just sort of got boiled back down, and I think that, you know, there was just so much homophobia, I mean, even in terms of working with guidance counsellors in schools who would only talk to me, and, like, it was constant, right? So, we could never get over this, like, hump of, like, being queer parents, to actually get the services and access.[8]

A few years ago, my colleagues Jeff Kugler and Nicole West-Burns at the Ontario Institute of Studies in Education created a framework for implementing equitable practices at school. The framework is called "Culturally Responsive and Relevant Pedagogy"[9] and is based on two big educational ideas from the United States: "Culturally Relevant Pedagogy"[10] and "Culturally Responsive Pedagogy."[11] The framework covers seven areas of equitable practice: 1) classroom climate and instruction; 2) school climate; 3) student voice and space; 4) family/caregiver-school relations; 5) school leadership; 6) community connections; and 7) culture of professional development. Of particular relevance to a discussion of Evan's comments is Jeff and Nicole's writing on family/caregiver-school relations. Here is Jeff and Nicole's list of the kind of practices that work towards creating equitable relationships between schools and families.

1. The school respects all families and family structures and invites them to participate in the life of the school and the educational process for the students.
2. The school does not use a top-down, one-sided approach in which the "professionals" need to inform the parents of how to best educate their children. To the contrary, the school uses a model that ensures true collaboration based on mutual respect.
3. The school recognizes and acknowledges that the parent community knows the most, and cares deeply about their children.
4. The school honours family/caregivers as an educational resource, by valuing their personal and/or professional knowledge of their children and by inviting them to share their areas of expertise with the students and school.
5. In communities where people have not always had the best experiences in school themselves, trust needs to be established and nurtured. It is incumbent upon the school to take the first steps.
6. Where necessary, the school seeks out services to allow another adult (for example, family member, legal guardian, community advocate) to act in the student's best interests.
7. Family/caregivers are consulted with and involved in making key decisions regarding important aspects of their children's school life.

8. The communication between teachers/administrators and family/caregivers is respectful and validating.
9. The forms of communication are invitational, accessible, multilingual, and timely.
10. The school uses innovative outreach strategies to make family/caregivers feel welcome.
11. The school recognizes the socio-political events that shape family/caregiver involvement. Changes in labour laws, housing policies, job restructuring and outsourcing, immigration policies, market fluctuations, etc. all have an impact. Therefore the school has reasonable and realistic expectations of family/caregiver time and resources.

Jeff and Nicole's list of practices is comprehensive. But if the school that Evan's oldest daughter had attended had been able to implement even one of the first three practices on the list – respect all families, collaborate with them, and acknowledge that parents know the most about their children – the difficulty of being queer, teenaged parents might have been mitigated somewhat and Evan's daughter might have received the special education services she needed. With the support of a special education program, Evan's daughter might not have dropped out of school in Grade 8 and might have gone on to complete high school.

In reviewing Jeff and Nicole's list, I looked for a practice that could respond to Nazbah's call in Letter 19 for support for parents who bully their own children. I couldn't find one. Perhaps, an additional practice could be added to practice 10. In addition to using innovative strategies to make family/caregivers feel welcome, the school could find ways to provide access to skill-building opportunities to parents who request them.

All the best,
Tara

Notes

1 Interview, June 19, 2017.
2 In this letter I use the term "living with autism" rather than the terms "autistic" or "autistic person." Many parents prefer the phrase "living with

autism" or "person with autism" over "autistic" because person-first language (putting the word "person" before any identifier such as "autism") emphasizes the humanity of their children. I understand that there are others in the autism community who prefer terminology such as "autistic" or "autistic person" because they understand autism as an inherent part of an individual's identity. In their interview, Evan and Jess never referred to their son as autistic. Once they referred to his autism and once they talked about him being in an autism program at his school. Following Evan and Jess's lead, I use the term "living with autism" to talk about their son.

3 Interview, June 19, 2017.
4 See https://www.autismspeaks.ca/about-autism/what-is-autism/.
5 Interview, June 19, 2017.
6 Interview, June 19, 2017.
7 Interview, June 19, 2017.
8 Interview, June 19, 2017.
9 See Kugler and West-Burns, 2010.
10 See Ladson-Billings, 2009, 2014.
11 See Gay, 2010.

LETTER 21

POLY FAMILIES

Dear Teacher:

Two of the families we have interviewed in the *LGBTQ Families Speak Out* project describe their families as poly families. "Poly" means many, and the phrase "poly families" refers to families with polyamorous parents. In the Addley family, there are three parents raising four children together (see Letter 9). In Evan and Jess's family there are three parents raising two children together (see Letter 20). Jess joined Evan's family a year before the interview took place. She is the newest parent in her family. Towards the end of our interview we asked Jess and Evan to talk about how their children's school responded to Jess's transition into the family.

JESS: . . . To identify as a poly family was still pretty new to me and, and I didn't know how the school system would take it. Um, and I think the first point of contact we made was [with] our son's school, and their welcoming and their willingness to understand it really helped me be able to settle into a poly family really well. Um, with our daughter's school, it just kind of happened, I don't really know, [it] just blossomed I guess. Um, but I think it felt real when I started to sign, you know, the kids' permission slips. Um, [the other two] got sick of filling out all the paperwork from school and I was like, "Oh my gosh, I get to parent."

EVAN: She was so new and excited to do that.

JESS: Yeah. And so I was able to do it. I think that is also what helped. The schools realized that there was another guardian at home because these forms were coming in, and we also sent a letter saying, um, that I would, that I would be able to sign the forms and pick the kids up and be involved in their life in a school capacity.

EVAN: I think, though, you touched on something important which was that, I mean, so, I sort of typed up a letter saying like, "Just so you know, we're giving her permission to sign forms and all that," but, I mean, there's really no policy within the [school board] around poly parents.

So, there's policies in place around, like, divorced parents and, I mean, yeah, I spend a lot of time researching, you know, like legal stuff, how parents go about that, and I think, you know, there was this piece around if a mom and a dad got divorced and the mom remarried then the mom and the stepdad could sign papers, but there wasn't anything that retained all three in that, and there was nothing to sort of set the precedent.

So, I mean, we're really lucky that the schools have honoured that, but I know from being a lesbian mom a long time ago [see Letter 20] that there was always a huge fight to get that recognition ... So, much [of this] has to do with family law, right? And in our legal system the fact that Jess has no legal rights to the children, the schools have been really good with recognizing [us], but it's complicated even in terms of being a special needs parent, you know, because she can't sign any medical forms. And so [she] still [has] no legal, no legal responsibility, in much the same way that my partner back in the '90s wasn't able to be recognized as a guardian.

TARA: So, legally, there's more work that needs to be done in order to have you fully, legally, legitimate, to have your parenting legitimized legally.

JESS: Yes.

EVAN: Yes, and I mean the law has changed because now you can have up to four people on a birth certificate. But it's not retroactive. So, for any of us that have kids born before, I think it's like last year, it's not retroactive, so we can't add parents on to the birth certificate ...

... I think, I mean, in many ways we're very much at the mercy of who the school administration is and the teachers. I know that, you know, I think we still – even though we're very out and definitely the schools' acceptance encouraged us to be out about being a poly family in lots of different situations – um, it's still always questionable about whether, whether it's the best idea. And I think we generally are out. We're out in our jobs, we're out at school, we're out at church ... [But] I mean it's very much still, I think, something in the back of our heads because there is no legal or human rights protection the way there is now for queer and trans folks.[1]

While both Jess and Evan talk about how welcoming their children's schools were, and how the schools' acceptance helped Jess settle into her new poly family, Evan reminds us that public school boards don't have any policies around poly parents, and poly families are "at the mercy" of the administration of their children's schools. As discussed in several of the letters in this book, not all school principals have been educated about the experiences of LGBTQ students and families, and not all principals are ready and able to support them.

As we began to end our interview, I asked Evan and Jess if there was anything else they wanted to say before we closed. Jess talked about the possible impact associated with the *LGBTQ Families Speak Out* project and Evan returned to the topic of needing to recognize and legitimize queer and poly families.

JESS: I'm really excited for your project. And I really hope that it has, um, a really big impact for the future teachers. Um, because they're getting a group of kids who are growing up in this kind of weird society where, you know, there's lots of identities around, there's lots of family makeups, community makeups, so they're really going to have to navigate themselves around what society has presented them and what community they're in at that point.

EVAN: I mean, it's especially important work, because I think sometimes in Toronto we think that, you know, we're so accepting and everything's great and, um, you look at the protests and stuff that happened around the sex ed. curriculum change[2] and I mean it just sort of drives home that, really, we still have to fight for our families to be recognized and legitimized and I think, like Jess said, the kids that are sort of coming into the school system now are growing up in such a different culture than, you know, someone our ages did in terms of queer acceptance. I mean, in our friend group, I'd say 80 percent of our friends are poly, right? And lots of them have kids and are raising kids together and so, I mean, it's just – it's so different than what it was, but the institutions that I think our families have to interact with, I mean, are still, I mean, it's going to take a long time to catch up.[3]

Here, both Jess and Evan argue that many of the children, youth, and families who are coming into the school system have grown up in a culture of queer acceptance that is different from the culture most parents, teachers, and principals grew up in. Some of the families that teachers will work with are going to be different from their own families. Serving them well will require an openness to difference. In Evan's words, teachers and schools who haven't yet worked with LGBTQ families will have to catch up.

All the best,

Tara

Notes

1 Interview, June 19, 2017.
2 As discussed in Letter 17, in September 2015 the Ontario Ministry of Education introduced an updated Health and Physical Education Curriculum. When the updated curriculum was introduced, several parent groups publicly opposed some of the additions, including new discussions on gender identity and sexual orientation. It is this opposition to which Evan is referring here. Despite some small but vocal parental opposition, the 2015 curriculum was taught in schools between 2015–2018. In the fall of 2018, the newly elected Conservative government in Ontario repealed the 2015 Health and Physical Education curriculum for elementary students and replaced it with an interim curriculum which includes sex education material created 20 years ago in 1998. The repeal of the 2015 curriculum speaks directly to Evan's point that LGBTQ families still have to fight to be recognized and legitimized.
3 Interview, June 19, 2017.

LETTER 22

EXPECTING LGBTQ FAMILIES AND STUDENTS AT SCHOOL

Dear Teacher:

In this last letter in Part 3 I want to share some thoughts on how teachers and principals can create schools where LGBTQ families and students are expected, accepted, supported, and not merely tolerated.

Garrett Metcalfe is a gay, Indigenous father who participated in our *LGBTQ Families Speak Out* project. He is also a teacher in an alternative high school that enrolls students who haven't been successful in mainstream schools. Garrett supports students in completing their high school diplomas. He has been teaching in alternative schools for 14 years of his 20-year teaching career, and says he ended up teaching in alternative schools because he didn't fit into mainstream schools. From the very beginning of his career, Garrett wanted to do equity-based, social justice education work, but when he first began working as a teacher in mainstream schools, there wasn't an openness to that kind of teaching. In fact Garrett told us that, when he first tried to establish a Gay Straight Alliance at his mainstream school, his job was threatened. So, Garrett moved to teaching in alternative schools where his equity-based work was welcome.

Garrett describes the students who are currently enrolled in his alternative school as marginalized. Many of them live in poverty, many of them identify as LGBTQ, and many are youth of colour. To create an inclusive curriculum for his students, Garrett teaches units on Black Studies, Men's Studies, Women's Studies, Native Studies, and Queer Studies. He says he thinks his school is the only public school in the province of Ontario that offers high school credit for

Queer Studies. When I asked Garrett why he thinks students have chosen to enroll in his school to finish their high-school education, he said mainstream schools are not meeting the needs of racialized and queer students. The students who find their way to his school are the ones who are most disengaged.

GARRETT: And the fact that they've walked through the door is huge for us … we can connect them [back to school]. Because they can see themselves in the curriculum, they tend to stay.

TARA: Tell us a little bit about the queer curriculum you offer, because most of the families that we've talked to say – and most of the students we've talked to say – there's very little representation of LGBTQ families or LGBTQ folks in their curriculum. What does your Queer Studies course look like?

GARRETT: Um, it is specifically catered and designed for the queer students. We get allies in the room, allies are more than welcome, but the purpose of creating it was to meet their [LGBTQ students] needs, to give them a safe space one period a day [where] they connect. So, when they enter the school, um, through self-identifications, whether being trans, or their sexual orientation, um, our [administrative] office is trained to hook them up with me. And then I try to engage them. If I'm not teaching the Queer Studies at the time, I track them while they're here to see how they're doing.

The actual Queer Studies curriculum for me is about identity and seeing themselves, and so [we spend] a lot of time around identity, terminology, who are you? How do you identify? Where is your place? Um, I do a lot of queer history with them in as well. It's a lot of sociology, right? Anti-oppression [education]. Learning to navigate – so, um, figuring out their identities and then learning to navigate a world that doesn't see them …

TARA: … You talked about a variety of courses that have a particular lens: Queer Studies, Black Studies, Native Studies. Um, how are you able to work with both particular identity focus and also engage with the idea of intersectionality? … [F]or example, there are LGBTQ students who also identify as Black, who also identify as Indigenous. Are there ways that teachers or that you yourself have found to create some kind of discussion of multiple identities at the same time as you are focusing on a particular identity?

GARRETT: Every one of our courses, and this isn't just me, um, our entire
staff is well-versed and trained on all these identities and so embed-
ding – and this is also part of my job in special programs, is working
with all of our teachers to embed all of the social justice – all of the
identities in all of our curriculum. It's not just in my room. So, when
[students] go from room to room they will hear the same terminology,
they have all done the Power Wheel[1] and their area of oppression and
understand those concepts of intersectionality. When they are doing
work in an English class, they are reading Indigenous novels, and
they're reading other books specific to identities and they can pick and
choose where those readings lie. And because we're a social activist-
based school and social activist-driven school, it happens in every
room. So, they understand these concepts of oppression in all of their
classes, they understand – so do the staff, the custodial [team]. It's our
entire building which is versed in this, so they're going to see their
identities not just in my room. They're going to see it in all of their
rooms.[2]

For Garrett, creating a school culture that expects and accepts
LGBTQ students and families means making sure LGBTQ and
other marginalized students see themselves represented in the curriculum, in every single one their classes.

The importance of creating schools where LGBTQ families and
students are expected can't be overestimated. In a powerful essay about
their own experience in school, benjamin lee hicks writes about the
violence and trauma of not being expected.

> When I think directly about my own experiences growing up in
> school and society, I know that every fibre of my queer/trans body
> remembers the depth of tired that comes from not understanding
> how to speak. *"I remember the futility of trying to splice together
> fragments of a language that was too limited to tell the story myself to
> anyone, including myself. It has taken a long time to learn that public
> education was not constructed to include those of us who exist in the in-
> between, and even longer to understand that this is not something we
> need to be ashamed of."*[3] **This** is essentially what I mean when I
> write about the experience – the violence – of not being expected
> ... To arrive into a system of education where you are excited to

play and grow and communicate, only to find that the words to describe the precious aspects of **who you are** at your core do not even exist according to the people who teach you is traumatic ... *and it stays.*[4]

Like the writing by Makeda Silvera in Letter 17, reading hicks' reflections on growing up in school and society is very painful. hicks tells us that not understanding how to speak about their gender created deep exhaustion. They also tell us how their excitement about going to school was shattered by a system that didn't – and still doesn't – include transgender and gender diverse children, children who exist "in-between" the binary categories of girl and boy. Finally, they tell us going to school was traumatic. And, the trauma has stayed with them.

To counter the shame and violence transgender and gender diverse children and youth experience at school, Garrett Metcalfe works to include queer identities and queer history in his curriculum. A little over ten years ago, in 2007, I wrote an article called "Safe, Positive and Queering Moments in Teaching Education and Schooling" with my colleagues Vanessa Russell and Andrea Daley.[5] In the article, we argued that teaching and learning about gender and sexuality at school could be characterized by three different kinds of moments: safe, positive, and queering moments. Safe moments are moments when individual incidents of bullying are addressed at school (see Letters 18 and 19) and when teachers, principals, and students share the general goal of promoting tolerance at their school. Positive moments at school happen when teachers not only address incidents of bullying but also promote acceptance by creating curriculum that challenges homophobic and transphobic ideas and represents a variety of LGBTQ lives with respect. Garrett's Queer Studies unit is an excellent example of teaching that works towards positive moments at school.

Queering moments, on the other hand, at school move beyond the positive representation of LGBTQ people by disrupting cisgender normativity and heteronormativity at school. They also work to promote an understanding of oppression as multiple, interconnected, and ever changing. When Garrett talks about how all the teachers at his school try to embed all of the identities of their students into curriculum and work to help their students understand concepts of intersectionality, power, and privilege, I see this work as creating queering moments at school. Other queering moments that have been discussed in this book include the moment when Violet Addley's teacher, Ms. Richards, encouraged her to put on the dress she had brought to school, and the moment when Jess Swance-Smith was acknowledged as a third parent by her school.

In the conclusion of our article, Vanessa, Andrea, and I write that we hope our safe, positive, and queering moments framework would serve as a guide for teachers who want to think more intentionally about the moments that might emerge from their teaching about gender and sexuality. Our framework resonates deeply with hicks' writing of (not) being expected at school and Max Redecopp's discussion of tolerance, acceptance, and support (recall Letter 3). Safe moments work towards tolerance at school: "I'll sit beside you." Positive moments work towards acceptance and support: "I'll put my arm around you" and "I'll lift you up when you can't get up." Queering moments, which work to challenge cisgender normativity and heteronormativity, however, show that teachers and principals have been expecting and have been preparing for the arrival of LGBTQ students and families at their school, like Garrett and his colleagues.

All the best,

Tara

Notes

1 The exercise Garrett refers to as the Power Wheel is similar to an exercise we use at OISE called the Power Flower. A description of the Power Flower exercise is available in an anti-racist education book for teachers called *Letters to Marcia* by Enid Lee (Lee, 1985). It is also available in *Educating for a Change* by a group of educators from the Doris Marshall Institute (Arnold et al, 1991) and on the OISE website: http://www.oise. utoronto.ca/edactivism/Activist_Resources/The_Power_Flower.html.

2 Interview, January 27, 2018.

3 See hicks, 2016.

4 See hicks, 2017.

5 See Goldstein, Russell, and Daley, 2007.

CONCLUSION: LETTER 23
TAKE-AWAYS

Dear Teacher:

Over the last few years, at the end of each of our classes, my students and I sit in a circle and share what we are each taking away from the discussions we had that day. "Take-Aways" give us an opportunity to reflect on an idea or practice that has mattered to us, provoked us in some way, and/or provided us with a new perspective on gender and sexuality.

In this last letter, I want to summarize the discussions I've included in this book by sharing my take-aways from the experience of writing letters to teachers about teaching gender and sexuality at school. Here, in no particular order of importance, is a list of some of the key ideas, practices, and perspectives I am taking away from the letters I have written to you.

1. LGBTQ students and families don't want to be tolerated. They want to be expected, accepted, and supported for who they are.
2. In order to do any good, equity policies that protect the rights of LGBTQ students and families have to be implemented.
3. Gay Straight Alliances help schools develop a culture that creates a safer and more supportive learning environment for LGBTQ students and families.
4. Teacher allyship makes a difference in the lives of LGBTQ students and families.
5. Allyship without action is an oxymoron.

6. Not everyone's gender identity aligns with the sex they were assigned at birth.
7. Not everyone identifies as a boy or a girl. There are boys, girls, and people who identity as both or neither.
8. When the words that describe transgender and gender diverse people do not even exist in the minds of teachers, the result is traumatic. And, the trauma stays.
9. Incidents of gender-based and homophobic bullying must be addressed in classrooms and schools.
10. Children and youth need support from adults to learn how to stop bullying.
11. Gender-based and homophobic bullying is not anti-social behaviour. It is social behaviour that polices gender and sexuality in school. To stop bullying in a substantial and sustained way, schools need to create curriculum that teaches students that there are many ways to express their gender and many ways to love.
12. Sex education is like visiting a carnival: you can never do it all in one day, and it can be fun and strange and sometimes a little scary.
13. Some people experience both racism and homophobia. We need to fight both together.
14. Indigenous students who take time to respond to questions in class are thinking about their answers.
15. We all need to learn about the impact of residential schools on generations of Indigenous and Two-Spirit students and families and acknowledge the harm we've done.
16. Gender is fluid and can change.
17. Sexuality is fluid and can change.
18. Parents and teachers need to listen to kids when they tell them how they feel about their gender.
19. People can identify as LGBTQ and Muslim, Catholic, Jewish, Anglican.
20. In 2016, the Anglican Diocese of Toronto elected its first openly gay bishop, Bishop Kevin Robertson, who is raising two children with his partner, Mohan Sharma.
21. Many children and youth are growing up in a culture of queer acceptance. Schools have to catch up.

22. Some children need to make more than one Mother's Day and Father's Day card.
23. Parents and children living in LGBTQ families make strategic decisions around when to come out and when not to come out.
24. Putting up posters supporting LGBTQ students and families without working to change school culture is like "putting lipstick on a pig."
25. Creating a school culture that expects, accepts, and supports LGBTQ students and families requires intentionality, advocacy, activism, allyship, a long-term commitment, and . . . love.

All the best,
Tara

References

Airton, L. (2016). Gender-neutral pronouns shouldn't be a big deal. *The Globe and Mail*, October 26, 2016. https://www.theglobeandmail.com/opinion/gender-neutral-pronouns-shouldnt-be-a-big-deal/article32497815/.

Arnold, R., Burke, B., James, C., Martin, D. and Thomas, B. (1991). *Educating for a Change*. Toronto: Between the Lines.

Brill, S. and Pepper, R. (2008). *The Transgender Child: A Handbook for Families and Professionals*. San Francisco, CA: Cleis Press.

Chasnoff, D. and Cohen, H. (Producers) (1996). *It's Elementary: Talking about Gay Issues in School*. San Francisco, CA: Women's Educational Media.

Coloroso, B. (2015). *The Bully, the Bullied, and the Not-So-Innocent Bystander: From Preschool to High School and Beyond*. New York, NY: Harper Collins.

Crenshaw, K. (1989). Demarginalizing the intersection of race and sex: A Black feminist critique of antidiscrimination doctrine, feminist theory and anti-racist politics. University of Chicago Legal Forum. Special issue*: Feminism in the Law: Theory*, Practice *and* Criticism, 139–168.

Crenshaw, K. (2016, October). *Kimberlé Crenshaw: The urgency of intersectionality*. [Video file] Retrieved from https://www.ted.com/talks/kimberle_crenshaw_the_urgency_of_intersectionality.

Cronn-Mills, K. (2012). *Beautiful Music for Ugly Children*. Woodbury, MN: Llewellyn Worldwide Ltd.

Diaz, E. M. and Kosciw, J. G. (2009). *The Experiences of Lesbian, Gay, Bisexual, and Transgender Students of Color in Our Nation's Schools*. New York, NY: GLSEN.

Dyck, R. (2012). *Outcomes and recommendations from the 2012 LGBTQ youth suicide prevention summit*. Toronto: Egale Canada Human Rights Trust (available at http://egale.ca/wp-content/uploads/2013/02/YSPS-Report-online.pdf).

Edwards, S. (2017). Five moving stories about what it's like to be a queer Muslim. *Toronto Life*, June 23, 2017. https://torontolife.com/city/life/five-moving-stories-like-queer-muslim/.

Epstein, R., Idems, B. and Schwartz, A. (2013). Queer spawn on school. *Confero: Essays on Education, Philosophy & Politics 1*(2): 173–208.

Fayngold, I. (Producer and Director) (2005). *Hineini: Coming Out in a Jewish High School*. Boston, MA: Keshet.

Gay, Geneva. (2010). *Culturally Responsive Teaching: Theory, Research, and Practice* (2nd edn). New York, NY: Teachers' College.

Goldstein, T. (2004). Performed Ethnography for Anti-Homophobia Teacher Education: Linking Research to Teaching. *Canadian On-Line Journal of Queer Studies in Education*, 1(1), 25 pages. http://jqstudies.library.utoronto.ca/index.php/jqstudies/article/view/3280.

Goldstein, T. (2010). *Snakes and Ladders*: A performed ethnography. *International Journal of Curriculum and Pedagogy 3*(1): 68–113.

Goldstein, T., Collins, A. and Halder, M. (2007). Anti-homophobia education in public schooling: A Canadian case study of policy implementation. *Journal of Gay and Lesbian Services, 19*(2): 47–66.

Goldstein, T., Russell, V. and Daley, A. (2007). Safe, Positive and Queering Moments in Teaching Education and Schooling: A Conceptual Framework. *Teaching Education Journal, 18*(3): 183–199.

Gustavson. M. and Schmitt, I. (2011). Culturally queer, silenced in school? Children with LGBTQ parents and the everyday politics of/in community and school. *Lambda Nordica 16*(2-3): 159–187.

hicks, b. l. (2016). Chapter 5: BEYOND THIS OR THAT: Challenging the Limits of Binary Language in Elementary Education Through Poetry, Word Art, and Creative Book Making. In s. j. Miller (ed.) *Teaching, Affirming and Recognizing Trans and Gender Creative Youth: A Queer Literacy Framework*. New York, NY: Palgrave MacMillan.

hicks, b. l. (2017). Gracefully unexpected, deeply present and positively disruptive: Love and queerness in classroom community. *Bank Street Occasional Paper Series 37* (Part III). New York, NY: Bank Street College of Education.

hooks, b. (2000). *All About Love; New Visions*. New York, NY: Harper Perennial.

I'm Here. I'm Queer. What the Hell Do I Read? (leewind.org).

Kann L., Olsen, E. O., McManus, T. et al. (2016). Sexual identity, sex of sexual contacts, and health-related behaviors among students in grades 9–12—United States and selected sites. *MMWR Surveillance Summaries, 65*(9): 1–202.

Kosciw, J., Greytak, E., Giga, N., Villenas, C. and Danischewski, D. (2015). *GLSEN: The 2015 national school climate survey*. New York, NY: GLSEN (available at www.glsen.org).

Kugler, J. and West-Burns, N. (2010). The CUS Framework for Culturally Responsive and Culturally Relevant Pedagogy. In C. Smith (ed.) *Anti-Racism in Education: Missing in Action. Our Schools Our Selves, 19*(3): 215–224. Available at: http://www.easywebdesignsolutions.com/georgemartell/email27/Culturtally_Engaged_Pedagogy.pdf.

Kumashiro, K. (ed.) (2001). *Troubling Intersections of Race and Sexuality: Queer Students of Color and Anti-Oppressive Education.* New York, NY: Rowman and Littlefield.

Ladson-Billings, G. (1995). But That's Just Good Teaching! The Case for Culturally Relevant Pedagogy. *Theory into Practice, 34*(3): 159–165.

Ladson-Billings. G. (2009). *The Dreamkeepers: Successful Teachers of African-American Children* (2nd ed). San Francisco, CA: Wiley.

Ladson-Billings, G. (2014). Culturally Relevant Pedagogy 2.0: a.k.a. the Remix. *Harvard Educational Review, 84*(1): 74–84.

Lee, E. (1985). *Letters to Marcia: A Teacher's Guide to Anti-Racist Education.* Toronto: Cross Cultural Communication Centre.

McCaskell, T. (2005). *Race to Equity: Disrupting Educational Equality.* Toronto: Between the Lines.

McNeilly, K. (2012). Beyond the "bedrooms of the nation": An interpretative phenomenological analysis of Canadian adolescents with lesbian, gay, or bisexual-identified parents. Unpublished PhD thesis, University of Toronto. https://tspace.library.utoronto.ca/bitstream/1807/34808/1/McNeilly_Kenneth_D_201211_PhD_thesis.pdf.

Payne, E. and Smith, M. (2012). Rethinking Safe Schools Approaches for LGBTQ Students: Changing the Questions We Ask. *Multicultural Perspectives*, 14: 187–193.

Payne, E. and Smith, M. (2013). LGBTQ kids, school safety, and missing the big picture: How the dominant bullying discourse prevents school professionals from thinking about systemic marginalization or . . . Why we need to rethink LGBTQ bullying. *QED: A Journal in GLBTQ Worldmaking*, 1: 1–36.

Pendleton Jiménez, K. (2016). *Tomboys and Other Gender Heroes: Confessions from the Classroom.* New York, NY: Peter Lang.

Reiff Hill, M. and Mays, J. (2013). *The Gender Book.* Houston, TX: Marshall House Press.

Ringrose, J. and Renold, E. (2010). Normative Cruelties and Gender Deviants: The Performative Effects of Bully Discourses for Girls and Boys in School, *British Educational Research Journal*, 36: 590.

Saewyc, E., Pyne, J., Frohard-Dourlent, H., Travers, R. and Veale, J. (2017). *Being Safe, Being Me in Ontario: Regional Results of the Canadian Trans Youth Health Survey.* Vancouver: Stigma and Resilience Among Vulnerable Youth Centre, School of Nursing, University of British Columbia. http://saravyc.sites.olt.ubc.ca/files/2017/10/SARAVYC_Trans-Youth-Health-Report_Ontario-WEB-FINAL.pdf.

Silvera, M. (1995). Confronting the "I" in the Eye: Black Mother, Black Daughters. In K. Arnup (ed.) *Lesbian Parenting: Living with Pride and Prejudice.* Charlottetown: Gynergy Books, pp. 311–320.

Silverberg, C. and Smyth, F. (2015). *Sex is a Funny Word.* New York, NY: Triangle Square.

Simon, R. (Producer), Baer, P. (Director), with Evis, S., Walkland, T., hicks, b. l., Douglas, V. and teachers and youth in the Addressing Injustices Project (2017). *Gender is Like an Ocean.* (Documentary film.) Toronto. https://vimeo.com/219151863 (password is "music").

Taylor, B. (Co-Director), Parkin, W. (Co-Director), and Pendleton Jiménez, K. (Writer). (2008). *Tomboy.* (Children's animated short film.) Canada: Coyle Productions. http://vimeo.com/10772672.

Taylor, C. and Peter, T., with McMinn, T. L., Elliott, T., Beldom, S., Ferry, A., Gross, Z., Paquin, S. and Schachter, K. (2011). *Every class in every school: The first national climate survey on homophobia, biphobia, and transphobia in Canadian schools.* Final report. Toronto: EGALE Canada Human Rights Trust.

The No Big Deal Campaign (http://www.nbdcampaign.ca).

They Is My Pronoun (http://www.theyismypronoun.com).

Toronto District School Board. (2000). *Equity Foundation Statement and Commitments to Equity Policy.* Toronto: Toronto District School Board. Available at http://www.tdsb.on.ca/HighSchool/Equityinclusion/Guidelinespolicies.aspx.

Truth and Reconciliation Commission of Canada. (2015). Calls to Action. Winnipeg, Manitoba. Available at www.trc.ca.

Vowel, C. (2012). Language, culture, and Two-Spirit identity. Âpihtawikosisan| *Law Language Life: A Plains Cree speaking Métis Woman Living in Montreal,* March 29, 2012. http://apihtawikosisan.com.

AN ANNOTATED LIST OF
FAVOURITE RESOURCES

Part 1: Sexuality at School

1. Cohen, H. and Chasnoff, D. (Producers) (1996). *It's Elementary: Talking about Gay Issues in School.* **San Francisco, CA: Women's Educational Media.**

In *It's Elementary,* documentary filmmakers Deborah Chasnoff and Helen Cohen examine the experiences of LGBTQ students, families, and teachers in elementary school. The film takes the point of view of the students who talk about how it might feel to be teased for having two moms and what happens when other kids yell "faggot" on the playground and teachers don't do anything about it. The original feature-length film is one hour and 20 minutes long, but there is a shorter version, 37 minutes long, which can be used for professional development workshops. I use the full-length film in my classes. Even though the film was completed in 1996, the issues it brings to light still need to be addressed today.

Davies, C. and Robinson, K. H. (2016). *Working It Out: An interactive resource for pre-service teachers, teachers and other professionals working with young people about homophobia and transphobia in schools.* **Young and Well Cooperative Research Centre, Melbourne.** (Copies of this resource can be downloaded from the Young and Well CRC website: youngandwellcrc.org.au)

Australian researchers and educators Cristyn Davies and Kerry Robinson have been researching the experiences of LGBTQ children and youth for many years. *Working It Out* is an interactive resource for pre-service teachers, teachers, and other professionals working with young people about homophobia and transphobia in schools. It includes a performed ethnography about the experiences of Australian LGBTQ youth, a facilitator's guide, and questions that promote critical discussion and reflection. As explained in my "Getting Acquainted" letter, a performed ethnography is a play script based on research findings. Like my own performed ethnography, *Snakes and Ladders* (included at the end of this book), *Working It Out* is intended to be read aloud and discussed by a group of educators. The critical questions provided by Davies and Robinson are excellent discussion starters.

2. GLSEN (Gay, Lesbian and Straight Educators Network) (glsen.org)
GLSEN (pronounced "glisten") is an organization that was founded in 1990 by a small group of American teachers in Massachusetts who wanted to improve the lives of LGBTQ students at school. Twenty-seven years later, GLSEN has grown into a leading national education organization focused on creating safer and more affirming schools for LGBTQ students. GLSEN conducts original research on K-12 education to provide teachers with ways of improving the experiences of LGBTQ students at school. It also creates resources for teachers to use, partners with other national education organizations to share their expertise, and supports students to do work in their own schools and communities. Their website contains an abundant amount of resources for teachers, students, and families.

3. *I'm Here. I'm Queer. What the Hell Do I Read?* (leewind.org)
Lee Wind's website, *I'm Here, I'm Queer. What the Hell Do I Read?* contains a list of contemporary books with lesbian, gay, bisexual, transgender, questioning, queer, and gender creative teen characters and themes. It also includes a list of books with characters who are LGBTQ family members. Each entry on the list has a description of the book. Some of the entries contain excerpts from the book or links to movies that have been adapted from the book.

Part 2: Gender at School

1. Pendleton Jiménez, K. (2016). *Tomboys and Other Gender Heroes: Confessions from the Classroom*. New York, NY: Peter Lang.
Tomboys and Other Gender Heroes is based on a research study of gender stories Karleen Pendleton Jiménez collected from about 600

children and youth in both urban and rural communities in Ontario, Canada. In the study, she asked children and youth questions such as: "Have you ever been told you're too girlish or two boyish? How did you respond? Did you hide or change? Rebel or hurt? Or did you gleefully celebrate your style?" In the book, Pendleton Jiménez shares their responses and provides lesson plans and pedagogical strategies for teachers to collect and analyse gender stories with their own students.

2. Reiff Hill, M. and Mays, J. (2013). *The Gender Book.* **Houston, TX: Marshall House Press.**
The Gender Book is written as a comic book with hand-drawn graphics and lots of colour. It is intended for readers of all ages, including adults, and works to educate people about gender, gender expression, and gender identities. It also works to challenge misunderstandings people have about gender and gender minority people. Topics include:

- What is gender?
- Gender generalizations
- Gender versus sex
- Biological brain differences
- Gender behavior in kids
- Gender across cultures
- Gender binaries versus a gender spectrum
- Masculine women
- Feminine men
- Androgynous people
- Male to female physical transitions
- Female to male physical transitions
- Cross-dressing
- Drag kings/queens
- People who are intersex
- People who are gender queer
- How to be an ally

3. Simon, R. (Producer), Baer, P. (Director), with Evis, S., Walkland, T., hicks, b. l., Douglas, V. and teachers and youth in the Addressing Injustices Project (2017). *Gender is Like an Ocean.* **(Documentary film).**

Toronto. (http://addressinginjustices.com/gender-is-like-an-ocean – the password is "music")

Gender is Like an Ocean is a documentary film that follows a group of Grade 8 school students and teacher education students as they read and discuss the book *Beautiful Music for Ugly Children* by Kristin Cronn-Mills (2012) together. In intergenerational groups, the students and new teachers work together to create arts-based projects in response to the book.

Beautiful Music for Ugly Children tells the story of an 18-year-old who has begun to socially transition from being Elizabeth to being Gabe. It's the end of the school year, and Gabe gets a dream job as a local radio DJ. Over the summer, some really great things happen for Gabe. His radio show develops a fan base and he gets asked out. But some bad things happen too. Gabe gets outed as transgender and faces violence. *Beautiful Music for Ugly Children* won the 2014 Stonewall Award from the American Library Association and a 2014 Independent Publisher Book Award. The documentation of the students' and teachers' work together demonstrates the kinds of deep conversation students and teachers can have around the topics of gender, gender transition, and gender violence.

4. Taylor, B. (Co-Director), Parkin, W. (Co-Director), and Pendleton Jiménez, K. (Writer) (2008). *Tomboy*. (Children's animated short film). Canada: Coyle Productions. (http://vimeo.com/10772672)

Tomboy is an animated 14-minute video written and produced for children from ages 5 to 9. The video tells the story of a 9-year-old Latina-Canadian girl named Alex (short for Alejandra) who is bullied for being a tomboy. After a nasty exchange during a soccer game, when Alex is told to get off the field and find a pretty dress to wear, she runs home in tears. Her mother comforts her and reassures Alex that she's great just the way she is. As the story unfolds there are several funny moments as Alex's classmates discuss what kind of clothing boys and girls can wear. For example, boys can wear red if it's dark red going on maroon, but if girls want to wear red shorts the shorts need to be light red, going on pink. *Tomboy* is based on Karleen Pendleton Jiménez's own experience growing up as a tomboy, and can be used in the classroom to discuss gender expression and bullying.

Part 3: LGBTQ Families at School

1. Epstein-Fine, S. and Zook, M. (eds.) (2018). *Spawning Genera-*
tions: Rants and Reflections on Growing Up with LGBTQ+ Parents.
Bradford: Demeter Press.
Spawning Generations is a collection of essays written by writers who
have grown up with LGBTQ parents. The experiences they write
about span six decades, from the 1960s to the 2010s. Editors Sadie
Epstein-Fine and Makeda Zook, who identify as queerspawn themselves, have curated a volume of "rants" and "reflections" that provide a
space for queerspawn to tell their own stories on their terms.

2. Coloroso, B. (2015). *The Bully, the Bullied, and the Not-So-*
Innocent Bystander: From Preschool to High School and Beyond. **New**
York, NY: Harper Collins.
First published in 2002, Barbara Coloroso's guide on bullying provides
parents, teachers, and principals with ways to both prevent and stop
bullying at school. In this updated edition of the book, Coloroso discusses
the three people who are involved in bullying: the bully who perpetrates
the harm; the bullied, who is the target (and who may become a bully);
and the not-so-innocent bystander. Not-so-innocent bystanders include
peers or siblings who either watch, participate in the bullying, or look
away, as well as adults who see bullying as "teasing" and don't stop it.
Coloroso then suggests ways to hold children who bully accountable for
their behaviour and ways to help them change their behaviour.

3. LGBTQ Families Speak Out (www.lgbtqfamiliesspeakout.ca)
The *LGBTQ Families Speak Out* website hosts interviews with families
who discuss their experiences in Ontario elementary, middle and high
schools. Topics under discussion include:

*   coming out and not coming out at school
*   bullying
*   transitioning at school
*   sex education
*   what happens on Mother's Day and Father's Day

4. PFLAG Canada (http://pflagcanada.ca) **and PFLAG USA** (https://
www.pflag.org)

PFLAG Canada and PFLAG USA are national organizations founded by parents who wanted to help themselves and their family members understand and accept their LGBTQ children. On the homepage of both the Canadian and American websites there is a button – "Get Help Now" – where people can find face-to-face support groups, online support for people, and a list of resources. The resource list is extensive and includes lists of LGBTQ religious organizations, health-care websites, and support services.

THE UNICORN GLOSSARY

(a most-definitely-not-comprehensive list of terms related to gender and sexuality - compiled by benjamin lee hicks, 2018.)

Section 1: Introduction and Origins

Introduction

As people who often grow up in situations where lives and loves like ours are not widely celebrated, queer folks have become very adept at telling our own stories. The language that has developed for this task is necessarily fluid and, as such, the words we claim to describe queer worlds and experiences change frequently. The title of "Unicorn Glossary" is a nod to that fluidity because, regardless of specific semantics and the big/small ways that these words will shift in form/meaning over time, queer lives will always be *magic*.

Origins

The content of this glossary is adapted from a variety of sources, including:

1. Bardwell, S. (2012). *Gender and Sexuality: A Not-Necessarily-Comprehensive List of Terms*. Toronto: Unpublished paper, University of Toronto.
   * This paper by Sookie Bardwell in turn credits the following references:
   - http://transwhat.org/glossary/
   - An Introduction to Trans* Terminology – Radical Intersections Consulting: radical.intersections@gmail.com

- http://www.genderspectrum.org/about/understanding-gender
- http://nodesignation.wordpress.com/definitions/
- http://www.geneseo.edu/safe_zone/terminology
- http://geneq.berkeley.edu/lgbt_resources_definiton_of_terms
- http://www.rainbowhealthontario.ca/admin/contentEngine/ contentDocuments/Gender_Independent_Children_final.pdf

When I reference Bardwell throughout this glossary, please assume that her words also encompass contributions from the other scholars and activists that she credits.

2. hicks, b. l. (2016). Beyond This Or That: Challenging the Limits of Binary Language in Elementary Education Through Poetry, Word Art and Creative Book Making. In s.j. Miller (ed.) *Teaching, Affirming and Recognizing Trans and Gender Creative Youth: A queer literary framework*. New York, NY: Palgrave MacMillan.
3. hicks, b. l. (2017a). Gracefully unexpected, deeply present and positively disruptive: Love and queerness in classroom community. In D. Linville (ed.) *Queering Education: Pedagogy, Curriculum, Policy*. Occasional Paper Series 37. Bank Street College of Education.
4. hicks, b. l. (2017b). *ALL-WAYS in Transition: De-sensationalizing Beliefs About Trans Identities in Schooling Through Participatory Action Research*. Master's Thesis. Retrieved from: https://tspace. library.utoronto.ca/handle/1807/79127.
5. Reiff Hill, M. and Mays, J. (2013). *The Gender Book*. Houston, TX: Marshall House Press.
6. Silverberg, C. and Smyth, F. (2015). *Sex is a Funny Word*. New York, NY: Triangle Square.
7. The Toronto District School Board (2014). *Guidelines for the accommodation of transgender and gender independent/non-conforming students and staff*. Retrieved from: http://www.tdsb.on.ca/ AboutUs/Innovation/GenderBasedViolencePrevention/Accom modationofTransgenderStudentsandStaff.aspx.
8. Vowel, Chelsea (Métis) (2012). Language, culture, and Two-Spirit identity. Âpihtawikosisan|*Law Language Life: A Plains Cree speaking Métis Woman Living in Montreal*, March 29, 2012. Retrieved from: http://apihtawikosisan.com/2012/03/language-culture-and-two-spirit-identity/.

9. Wilson, Alexandria (Opaskwayak Cree Nation) (2015). Two-Spirit people, body sovereignty, and gender self-determination. *Red Rising* Magazine, September 21, 2015. Retrieved from: http://redrisingmagazine.ca/two-spirit-people-body-sovereignty-and-gender-self-determination/.
10. Youth, G. C. (2016). Glossary of terms: defining a common queer language. *Teaching, Affirming, and Recognizing Trans and Gender Creative Youth: A Queer Literacy Framework*, 299.

Section 2: What Do All Those Acronyms Mean?

As Tara explained in Letter 1: "Getting Acquainted," we use the initialism LGBTQ (lesbian, gay, bisexual, trans, and queer) to include people who identify as transgender, transsexual, Two-Spirit, questioning, intersex, asexual, pansexual, ally, agender, gender queer, gender variant, and/or pangender. You may have encountered a different configuration of this acronym in a different context, and you will likely continue to experience these variations in the future. These discrepancies can feel confusing and even alienating, but it is important to remember that it's nobody's fault: it's just that the terminology of queerness is always changing. These words that we use to describe ourselves are as fluid as identity is naturally in the ebb and flow of humanity, and it is okay to just let yourself have fun with that. All the terms listed above are explained in more detail throughout the subsequent sections of this glossary, but, before we begin, here are two additional variations that are (currently) in more common use.

LGBTTQQ2SA+: This acronym may affectionately be referred to as "alphabet soup" and represents a variety of sexual and gender identities, including lesbian, gay, bisexual, transsexual, transgender, queer, questioning, Two-Spirit, and allies. The plus sign (or asterisk*) at the end is intended to encompass other queer identity markers that have not been specifically named. It is often shortened to the more memorable "LGBTQ," in which the "Q" stands in for all of the letters that are not specifically listed (TDSB, 2014; Bardwell, 2012). Some variations to this model include "I" for intersex. More information about intersex identities can be found in this glossary; including the fact that, while some intersex folks *do* identify themselves as queer, many others do not.

QUILTBAG: This is another acronym that some people use to refer to a selection of sexual and gender identities including queer/questioning, undecided, intersex, lesbian, transgender/transsexual, bisexual, ally/asexual and gay/genderqueer. It is intended to be both more flexible and more memorable than some other versions of the acronym landscape.

Section 3: What is the Difference Between Gender, Sex, and Sexual Orientation?

Gender: "Gender, or the lack thereof, is part of a person's identity" (Reiff Hill & Mays, 2013). It is an idea that originates in personal thought and feeling, but it is also important to consider the ways that our own relationships *to* these ideas are socially constructed. Gender is personal. It is the way that you think and feel about yourself in relation to binary social definitions such as "male" and/or "female," and your gender may also include a rejection of or variation on these ideas (hicks, 2017b). "Social ideas about gender stem from societal expectations of how a person should behave based on their sex" (TDSB, 2014). "Societal expectations may vary by culture and consist of the attitudes, feelings, and behaviours that are associated with being female or male (Bardwell, 2012).

Sex: Includes physical (but still subjective) indicators such as external genitalia, internal reproductive structures, chromosomes, hormone levels, and secondary sex characteristics like breasts, facial or body hair, and patterns of body fat distribution. These characteristics are frequently assumed to be absolute and objective because medical models are fond of quantifying and sorting them into two discrete categories (male and female). In reality, sex is a continuum. The majority of people exist somewhere close to the ends of this continuum that we have named "male" and "female," but there is also a vast middle space occupied by *intersex* persons (TDSB, 2014).

Sexual orientation: Refers to someone's desire in relation to intimate, emotional, and sexual relationships with other people. This may be a lack of attraction to people of any gender (asexual); attraction to people of the same gender in a binary context (homosexual, gay, lesbian); to people of the opposite gender (heterosexual, straight); of either binary gender (bisexual); or, to people of any gender identity, including those that exist outside of a binary system (pansexual, polysexual, omnisexual, queer). This attraction may remain static, but it may also be fluid and change over time. When we talk about sexual orientation we are largely discussing one's attraction to other people of certain gender identities and expressions. However, individuals may also hold preferences for certain physical bodies, including certain primary and secondary sexual characteristics. Others still are attracted primarily to the way another person's brain works (sapiosexual) (Bardwell, 2012; hicks, 2017b).

Section 4: More About Gender

Gender identity: A person's inner sense of being male, female, neither, both, or something else entirely (genderfluid, genderqueer, etc.) It is important to remember that, since gender identity is internal, a person's gender identity is not necessarily visible to others. It is also not necessarily related to a person's medically assigned sex (Bardwell, 2012) or to their gender expression.

Gender expression: "The performance of one's own gender, especially how it is communicated to others through behavior, clothing, haircut, voice, and other forms of presentation" (Reiff Hill and Mays, 2013). It is also important to remember that "a person's gender expression may or may not reflect their gender identity" (Bardwell, 2012).

Personal gender: "You know all that boy/girl stuff you learned growing up? The pink and blue, the dolls and trucks, the tutus and ties? That's how your culture defines gender. There are expectations about the way you should look (and behaviours and interests you should have) if you have a particular kind of body. For example, there were rules about what was a 'boy' haircut or a 'girly' colour where I grew up. These can change over time and from place to place. Can you think of a time when you felt limited by your culture's ideas about your gender? Your *personal gender* is where you find yourself in this system. Maybe your body is like other boys' bodies and you see yourself as a boy and you act in the world like other boys, well, that's your gender. There are tons of ways to be a girl or a boy, and tons of options between and all around these. You don't have to choose. Your gender is where you feel most comfortable and it can grow and change, just like the rest of you. It can include your understanding of your physical body, your understanding of your inner self, and the way you express that unique self to the world. They are all facets of your own unique gender." (Reiff Hill and Mays, 2013).

Gender binary: A common system of thought which presumes that all people's gender identity fits into two rigidly fixed categories: male or female. In this system, gender identity is also assumed to correlate with assigned sex (Bardwell, 2012).

Non-binary gender: Understands gender as a broader, less defined, more fluid, and more imaginative/expressive matrix of ideas. It challenges power differentials by deconstructing and reconstructing ideas, reflecting on disjunctures, unpacking gender, gender identities and gender expressions, and providing opportunities for new knowledges to emerge (Youth, 2016).

*Additional reference for further options: *The Gender Book* (Reiff Hill and Mays, 2013).

*Related: *ENBY* is a current, pop culture short-form for non-binary (as in N-B).

Gender diversity: This term is used to recognize that many people's preferences and variations for self-expression do not fit within a binary gender system. Gender diversity refers to the multiple ways in which identities fall outside of commonly understood gender norms. It is also intended to remind us that diversity in identity and expression is a fundamental aspect of being human.

*Related: gender diverse *(GD)*

Gender spectrum: The gender spectrum presents a more nuanced way of viewing gender, and includes a wider range of possibilities for gender identity and expression. This way of thinking about gender recognizes that there is a complex relationship between gender and physical sex, and that being born with certain physical characteristics does not guarantee a particular gender identity (Bardwell, 2012). Some people also prefer to envision "gender" as multi-dimensional and/or decidedly non-linear (hicks, 2017a).

Gender roles: The socially constructed and culturally specific expectations around behaviour and appearance that are imposed on "women" and "men" in a binary gender system. These include expectations about behaviour, thoughts, and even feelings. These restrictions are based on the assumption that a person's gender identity will correlate with the sex they are assigned at birth (Bardwell, 2012).

Masculinity: Refers to the qualities that are typically ascribed to men in a given society, and that are considered to be socially appropriate behaviours, thoughts, and feelings for a "man" (Bardwell, 2012).

Femininity: Refers to the qualities that are typically ascribed to women in a given society, and that are considered socially appropriate behaviours, thoughts, and feelings for a "woman" (Bardwell, 2012).

Femme: The word femme is derived from the French word for woman. In the past it was used to refer to the more feminine-presenting member of a queer coupling. However, it is now most frequently used to describe the purposeful affectation of gender expression or behaviour that would traditionally be considered "womanlike" or feminine in a given culture by individuals of any gender identity. Increasingly this identity is claimed as a reaction against the devaluing of femininity within a patriarchal culture, and as an assertion that femininity can be considered a sign of strength (Bardwell, 2012). In a queer context, it is important to recognize that femme shaming can also be a particular problem in gay male and trans masculine communities.

Butch: In the past, butch was used to describe the more masculine-presenting member of a queer coupling. Currently, however, it is most frequently used to describe the purposeful affectation of gender expression or behavior that would traditionally be considered "manlike" or masculine in a given culture by individuals of any gender identity (Bardwell, 2012).

Gender conforming: A person may be described as "gender conforming" when their gender expression correlates with the sex that they were assigned at birth and/or that other people read them as. In this context, "conforming" means that one's personal gender expression is externally judged to "fit" the social norms of a given culture. There are multiple layers of social privilege involved in whether a person is seen to "conform" or not. The concept of "choice" in regards to conformity is also a construct of power and privilege.

Gender variant/Nonconforming: Expressing gender in a way that does not fit the dominant social expectations of a given culture in regards to dress, actions, and expression. These ideas are also very culturally specific and change/shift over time.

Gender independent: A term that is most widely used to refer to children whose gender identity and/or gender expression differs from what is culturally expected of their assigned sex. Gender independent children may strongly and consistently identify with a gender that differs from the one culturally connected to their assigned sex, or may express a gender identity that blends aspects of multiple genders and is fluid or changing. Some may be comfortable in their assigned sex while also expressing themselves in ways that do not conform to social norms.

*Not all gender independent children choose to identify as transgender, queer, etc. as they age (hicks, 2017a; Bardwell, 2012).

*Related: gender creative

Genderqueer: This is a relatively recent term that was coined and is used most frequently by people who experience a very fluid sense of both their gender identity and their sexual orientation and who do not want to be constrained by absolute or static concepts. Instead, genderqueer people prefer to be open to relocating themselves on continuums of gender and sexual orientation (hicks, 2017a; TDSB, 2014).

*Related: gender fluid

Genderf*ck: Refers to a conscious (and often celebratory) effort to "f*ck with", play with, and/or deconstruct traditional notions of gender identity, gender roles, and gender expression (Bardwell, 2012).

Genderless/Agender/Non-gender: Refers to individual people who do not identify with any gender.

Androgyny: A term that comes from the Greek words "andras" (meaning man) and "gyne" (meaning woman), and which refers to a mixing of masculine and feminine characteristics. This term is most commonly applied to gender expression (Bardwell, 2012).

Ambigender: This term is sometimes used by people with an undefined sense of gender (Bardwell, 2012), whether this be both "female" and "male" within a binary system or as an entirely other combination of gender ideas.

Third gender: This is a more formal and (in recent years/in some countries) legal term that is used to refer to people who identify as neither "male" nor "female". There are currently multiple countries around the world that legally recognize a third personal gender identity, but it is also important to know that these laws have varying political motivations and do not always translate into actual support and safety for queer expressions and/or individual human rights. Some current examples of these countries include Canada, USA, UK, Australia, New Zealand, India, Nepal, Pakistan, and Thailand.

Two-Spirit/2-Spirit: This term was developed in 1990 during the third annual inter-tribal First Nations Gay and Lesbian American Conference in Winnipeg. It is used by some First Nations people in place of the many other words one might use to describe sexual orientation and/or gender identity and expression. Often, Two-Spirit/2-Spirit identities are spoken about as though they have been uniformly celebrated and revered in all aboriginal cultures, but this erases a great deal of nuance in the way that these individuals are viewed and treated both in their own tribes and within a colonial framework (Vowell, 2012; Bardwell, 2012).

Additional notes about Two-Spirit/2-Spirit identity and terminology:

> *"I have been trying to find Cree-specific terms for Two-Spirit identities for many years ... Learning the words is not enough, however. Digging deeper and trying to understand the way that native peoples viewed Two-Spirited individuals is also important ... Reclaiming our traditions is more than learning our languages, but our languages do give us a 'way in' that absolutely should be explored. Overcoming colonially imposed views of sex, sexuality, gender and identity is no small matter, particularly since indigenous peoples are still experiencing colonialism in a very real way. We are not living in post-colonial times, no matter what Canadian politicians wish to claim."*
>
> (Vowell, 2012)

> *"There is much work to be done, then, to undo the work that has been done upon us. When we call ourselves Two-Spirit people, we are proclaiming sovereignty over our bodies, gender expressions and sexualities. "Coming in" does not centre on the declaration of independence that characterizes "coming out" in mainstream depictions of the lives of LGBTQI people. Rather, coming in is an act of returning, fully present*

in our selves, to resume our place as a valued part of our families, cultures, communities, and lands, in connection with all our relations. Indigenous sovereignty over our lands is inseparable from sovereignty over our bodies, sexuality and gender self-expression."

(Wilson, 2015)

Additional references regarding Two-Spirit/2-Spirit identity and terminology:

Fieland, K. C., Walters, K. L. and Simoni, J. M. (2007). "Determinants of Health Among Two-Spirit American Indians and Alaska Natives," pp. 268–300. In I. H. Meyer and M. E. Northridge (eds.) *The Health of Sexual Minorities.* New York, NY: Springer.

National Center for Transgender Equality (2012). "Injustice at Every Turn: American Indian and Alaskan Native Respondents in the National Transgender Discrimination Survey" (Washington, DC).

Wilson, A. (2008). "N'tacimowin inna nah': Our coming in stories." *Canadian Women Studies,* 26 (3–4). 193–199.

*For the history of the term Two-Spirit please see: http://www.twospiritmanitoba.ca/about.html.

Transition: The multifaceted process whereby some trans people change their appearance and body structures to better match their internal (gender) identity, and/or transition socially to live their lives more publicly in accordance to their personal gender identity. Transition may include: coming out to one's family, friends, and/or co-workers; changing one's name and/or sex marker on legal documents; hormone therapy; and possibly (though not always) some form of surgery (Youth, 2016; The Toronto District School Board, 2014). It is no one else's place to assume or suggest that someone will "complete" this process at any particular time: an individual's transition is finished if and when they decide, and may not include going through all of the aforementioned steps.

Social transition: This is the facet of gender transition in which other people become aware of an individual's personal gender identity, including their preferred name, pronoun, and the part(s) of the gender spectrum they most identify with. Ideally, a trans person's social transition is self-initiated and can progress at whatever pace and in whatever form feels most comfortable to them.

Transgender: A person whose sense of their own gender identity differs from the biological sex that they were assigned at birth (hicks, 2016; 2017a).

Cisgender: While trans is a Latin prefix meaning "the other side of", cis- is "the same side of." A cisgender person is someone whose gender identity and expression match the social expectations for the physical/biological sex they were assigned at birth, based on a binary, medical perception of their sex chromosomes, gonads, reproductive chromosomes, and external genitalia.

Transsexual: This term is usually differentiated from the definition for transgender with the clarification that *most* people who identify as transsexual use hormone treatments and/or surgeries to change their secondary sex characteristics and/or other aspects of their physical bodies to match their personal gender identity. Many transsexuals also identify with a more binary, male/female concept of gender. As with much gender-related terminology, however, these points are not *always* true. Both hormones and surgery are age, access, and cost prohibitive and, as such, some people who identify as transsexual have not begun any of these treatments. Similarly, some trans people who *have* accessed hormones/surgeries choose not to use this word because it feels connected to more exclusionary ideas of gender/transition/identity.

Trans: Is sometimes used as an umbrella term to include transgender identifying people and transsexuals as well as other gender diverse individuals (TDSB, 2014). Some of these individuals may choose to use "trans" as a shorthand way to refer to themselves.

FTM/F2M (Female to Male): This term is (most commonly) used to refer to individuals who were assigned a female sex at birth but who identify as male and as having transitioned (Bardwell, 2012).

MTF/M2F (Male to Female): This term is (most commonly) used to refer to individuals who were assigned a male sex at birth but who identify as female and as having transitioned (Bardwell, 2012).

Transfeminine: Used to describe a wide range of non-cisgender people whose gender identity falls on the feminine side of the gender spectrum (Bardwell, 2012).

Transmasculine: Used to describe a wide range of non-cisgender people whose gender identity falls on the masculine side of the gender spectrum (Bardwell, 2012).

Drag: Refers to a performative (and often celebratory) social expression of gender, during which a person may (or may not) also take on a specific persona by dressing in the clothing, hairstyle, and make-up of a gender identity other than that with which they usually identify. This performance is usually formulated with reference to a binary system of gender. As such, drag kings are generally feminine-identified people performing masculine gender, and drag queens are generally masculine-identified people performing feminine gender.

Section 5: Medical Terminology Related to Gender/Gender Identity

Gender reassignment surgery (GRS)/Sexual reassignment surgery (SRS): Refers to several types of operations that a person might choose to undergo in order to align their physical gender expression with their personal gender identity. These surgeries may include (but are not limited to) "top surgery" (breast augmentation or removal) and "bottom surgery" (altering genitals).

*Please also note that this is medicalized terminology and most trans people now use/prefer the term **"gender confirming surgery"** instead of GRS/SRS because it recognizes that one's gender does not change in the event of surgery: rather, it is something that can help to make their internal sense of gender more apparent/visible to others.

Non-op: Short form of "non-operation." This term is used to describe people who don't plan to undergo any surgery related to their trans identity. There are a variety of reasons why someone might make this decision, including (but not limited to) difficulties in accessing medical care (whether these be financial, institutional, or social), discontent with the available options or potential results, or a simple lack of desire.

*Related: **Pre-op** is a short form of pre-operation. This term is used to describe people who wish/plan to have surgery but who have not yet undergone these procedures (Bardwell, 2012). **Post-op** is a short form of post-operation. This term is used to describe people who have undergone all the sex reassignment surgery that they plan to undergo (Bardwell, 2012). It is important to remember that this terminology is deeply personal and is nobody's business other than the person whose body these experiences belong to.

- A trans person may refer to *themselves* with this terminology, but it is not up to anyone else to assume, ask about, label, or share any information about someone's surgery/ies.

Gender identity disorder: In recent times this was the language used by the DSM4 (Diagnostic and Statistical Manual for Mental Disorders – Fourth Edition) and the American Psychiatric Association to diagnose the binary, medicalized concept of "gender dysphoria" (GD). In 2013 the new DSM5 shifted this language for adult individuals but maintained that exact definition in relation to the experience of children. In both cases, "dysphoria" is assumed to be something synonymous with all transgender lives and as a "given" thing that all trans people experience. In other words, "if you identify as trans or GD, you must also be dysphoric." There is a dark and painful history attached to this diagnosis for trans/GD individuals (see article/link in Pyne, 2015[1]). For one, this diagnosis was (until as recently as four years ago in the province of Ontario) required by the medical establishment in order for trans people to access the medical care they might desire as part of their transition process, including hormonal therapy and/or surgical procedures. Still, today, the socially constructed concept of "gender dysphoria" remains a psychiatric-gatekeeper diagnosis that allows institutions to control individual access to medical care and coverage.

Section 6: UNgendering Language is Fun!

Chosen pronouns (sometimes: preferred pronoun): The pronouns that one feels most comfortable with when being spoken of or referred to. Non-binary examples might include: "ze," "per," "they," or "hir" (Youth, 2016; Reiff Hill and Mays, 2013). The best way to figure out what pronouns someone uses is to ask respectfully, with consideration and awareness as to whether the space in which you are asking would feel safe, supportive, and *queered* enough for the person to be comfortable answering you.

Additional references regarding pronouns:

Reiff Hill, M. and Mays, J. (2013). *The Gender Book*. Houston, TX: Marshall House Press.

They Is My Pronoun, at http://theyismypronoun.com/.

The No Big Deal Campaign (nbdcampaign), at http://www.nbdcam
paign.ca/.

- NBD badge and infographics, at http://www.nbdcampaign.ca/
  shareable-things.

Section 7: More About Sex (as a Noun)

Primary sex characteristics: Any of the physical structures in an animal
body that are related to reproduction from an evolutionary stand-
point. These include the testes, ovaries, and external genitalia.

Secondary sex characteristics: Any of the physical traits in a sexually
mature animal that are (medically considered to be) specific to one
sex in a binary system, but which are not directly part of the
reproductive system. The appearance of secondary sex characteristics is determined by the presence of sex hormones such as
estrogen, progesterone, and testosterone. In humans, secondary
sex characteristics can include traits such as facial hair or an
Adam's apple, which are generally assumed to code for "maleness,"
and breasts, which are generally assumed to code for "femaleness"
(Bardwell, 2012).

Assigned sex: The sex one is assigned at birth based on (binary medical
perceptions of) genitalia (Youth, 2016).

FAAB: Female-assigned-at-birth. An acronym referring to individuals
who were assigned female in sex at birth (Bardwell, 2017).

MAAB: Male-assigned-at-birth. An acronym referring to individuals
who were assigned male in sex at birth (Bardwell, 2017).

UAAB: Unassigned-at birth. An acronym that is used to refer to
individuals who were not assigned a sex at birth. This is a very rare
designation since attending physicians (and parents) almost always
choose to assign visibly intersex babies as either male or female at
birth (Bardwell, 2017).

*To learn more about the historical (and current) human rights viola-
tions facing intersex people as a result of medical/social assumptions,
please see http://www.isna.org/faq/concealment.

Intersex: Intersex is a socially constructed category that reflects real (and relatively common) biological variation. "Intersex" is a general term used for a variety of conditions in which a person is born with a reproductive or sexual anatomy that doesn't seem to fit the typical medical definitions of female or male. For example, a person might be born appearing to be female on the outside but having mostly male-typical anatomy on the inside. Or a person may be born with genitals that seem to be in-between the usual male and female types. Another intersex person may be born with mosaic genetics, so that some of their cells have XX chromosomes and some of them have XY. Although we generally speak of intersex as an inborn condition, intersex anatomy doesn't always show up at birth. If you ask experts at medical centres how often a child is born so noticeably atypical in terms of genitalia that a specialist in sex differentiation is consulted, the number comes out at about 1:1,500–2,000 births. But a lot more people than that are born with subtler forms of sex anatomy variations – some of which won't show up until later in life. Sometimes a person isn't found to have intersex anatomy until they reach the age of puberty or beyond (www.isna.org).

*It is also important to note that the "I" is no longer specifically included in most LGBTQ+/related acronyms due to differing opinions within the intersex community regarding the "queerness" of their experiences. For example, intersex is the only term in the LGBTQ+ range that does not originate in a self-selected/self-identifying way for the individual. Much more frequently it begins without their consent, at birth, as a medical diagnosis by doctors in consultation with parents/guardians.

Section 8: More About Sexual Orientation and Attraction (+ Sex as a Verb)

Queer: (1) Originally "queer" was a derogatory label used to refer to lesbian and gay people. More recently this term has been reclaimed by some (but not all) gay, lesbian, bisexual, and other non-heterosexual people as an inclusive and positive way to identify themselves. Many people now specifically identify as queer in addition to or instead of gay, lesbian, bisexual, etc. (Bardwell, 2012). (2) In a way that is neither always the same nor completely separate from sexuality, "queer" has also been adopted by many people who identify as other-than-cisgender on a spectrum of gender diversity. For example, see genderqueer (hicks, 2017a).

Homosexual: Sexual, emotional, and/or romantic attraction to people of the same gender in the context of a binary system.

Bisexual: A person who is attracted to two sexes or two genders within a binary gender system, but not necessarily simultaneously or equally. This term does not recognize the many other possible non-binary gender identities and expressions (Bardwell, 2012).

Pansexual/Polysexual/Omnisexual: Sexual, emotional, and/or romantic attraction to people of all genders. Pansexual/polysexual/omnisexual are used as alternatives to bisexual, which restricts gender to a binary and does not recognize the possibility for attraction to (or from) individuals who define their gender outside of the dominant binary system of male or female.

Asexual: A person who does not experience sexual attraction to people of any gender. An asexual person may still experience romantic feelings for other individuals.

*Related: **Ace** is a popular slang term used to describe someone with an asexual orientation (Bardwell, 2012).

Demisexual: A person who does not experience *primary* sexual attraction (such as a reaction to how someone looks, dresses, and carries themselves), but who does experience *secondary* sexual attraction once they've developed strong emotional relationships (Bardwell, 2012).

Aromantic: A person who is does not experience romantic feelings for people of any gender. An aromantic person may still experience sexual feelings for other individuals (Bardwell, 2012).

Romantic/Affectional orientation: This term refers to a person's feelings of romantic attraction to other people. For people who experience sexual attraction, romantic/affectional orientation determines which gender(s) they find themselves sexually attracted to. For people who are asexual, romantic/affectional orientation determines which gender(s), if any, a person experiences romantic feelings towards (Bardwell, 2012).

Primary sexual attraction (or primary sexual desire): Is the type of sexual attraction that originates in how someone looks, dresses, carries themselves, etc.

Secondary sexual attraction: Is the type of sexual attraction that develops over time based on a person's relationship with, and emotional connection to, another person (Bardwell, 2012).

Sexual behaviour: This term refers to the sexual activities that a person chooses to engage in with others. For various reasons, a person's sexual behaviour may or may not be connected to the sexual orientation with which they identify (Bardwell, 2012).

Section 9: Queering Ideas About Family and Intimate Relationships

Queerspawn: Individuals who are raised in a family with LGBTQ+ parent(s)/caregivers.

Monogamous: The preference for and practice of having a single sexual/romantic partner during a particular relationship/period of time (Bardwell, 2012).

Polyflexible: This term is used to express a personal openness to consensually non-monogamous relationship structures and is most often used by people who are also comfortable with being in a monogamous relationship structure (Bardwell, 2012).

Polyamorous: "Poly" means many and "amory" means love. Polyamory therefore refers to the practice of consensual non-monogamy and includes a wide variety of potential relationship and family structures (Bardwell, 2012).

Polyfidelitous: An intimate relationship structure where all members are considered equal partners in a secure relationship and agree to maintain relational intimacy solely with other members of this group.

Section 10: Other Important (But Admittedly Less Sparkly) Realities

Homophobia: The fear, hatred, and/or intolerance of people who are homosexual and/or who express themselves in ways that challenge traditional gender roles. Homophobia may stem from a fear of associating with gay and lesbian people and/or of being perceived as gay or lesbian. Homophobic behaviours can range from (and beyond) telling jokes about lesbian/gay/queer people to physical violence against people thought to be lesbian/gay/queer.

Biphobia: The fear, hatred, and/or intolerance of people who are bisexual by people of any sexual orientation. These feelings/behaviours are often directed towards bisexual people from both heterosexual and homosexual identified people (Bardwell, 2012).

Bi-erasure/Bi-invisibility: Bisexual erasure/bisexual invisibility occurs when the legitimacy of bisexuality (either in general or individually) is questioned and/or denied outright. The implications of this negation of identity may be social, emotional, and/or physical if access to health information/care is restricted (Bardwell, 2012).

Transphobia: A fear and/or hatred of transgender people. Transphobia can manifest in a variety of ways, including verbal and physical violence, harassment, and discrimination (Bardwell, 2012). These feelings/behaviours are often directed towards transgender people from cisgender people of various sexual orientations.

Trans-misogyny: The intersection of transphobia and misogyny that transfeminine people frequently encounter and transmasculine people do not (and/or are themselves responsible for perpetuating).

Misogyny: Feelings and actions connected to the hatred of women (trans and/or cis identifying).

Femmephobia: The hatred and/or fear of all things feminine. Femmephobia differs from misogyny in that it may be directed towards people of any gender identity who express characteristics that would traditionally be considered "feminine" in a binary gender system (Bardwell, 2012). For example, femmephobia also affects some feminine-presenting FAAB people and some cisgender men.

Sexism: Prejudice, stereotyping, and/or discrimination based on a person's socially perceived sex. In a patriarchal system, sexism is most commonly directed towards women or people read as female (Bardwell, 2012).

Cissexism: The assumption that all people will identify with the gender identity that corresponds to the sex that they were assigned at birth, and that a cisgender person's gender is more authentic, "real", natural, or desirable than a trans/GD person's gender (Bardwell, 2012).

Heterosexism: The societal/cultural, institutional, and individual beliefs and practices which assume that heterosexuality is the only natural, normal, and acceptable sexual orientation. In a heterosexist culture, everyone is assumed to be heterosexual until they "come out" as being otherwise (Bardwell, 2012).

Heterosexual privilege: The benefits and advantages that heterosexual people (and/or people that are read as heterosexual) receive in a heterosexist culture.

Privilege: A right or immunity that is granted by/to members of a dominant group based on certain characteristics, including membership or assumed membership, in the dominant group. For example, a trans man may be granted male social privileges based on the way that his male gender expression is read by others (Bardwell, 2012).

Passing: This term can be used in regards to both sexuality and gender. When it is used in regards to sexuality, it usually means that a non-straight person passes as heterosexual in their day-to-day life. In regards to gender, it usually means that someone performs their gender in such a way that the general public does not question that they are "really" of the gender (within the gender binary) they appear to be (Bardwell, 2012; hicks, 2017a).

*Many trans people prefer the terminology "read as" as opposed to "passing as" because this takes the (conceptual) responsibility off that individual to perform in a certain acceptable way, and indicates that it is actually external social perceptions that determine how one is seen/understood.

Passing privilege: In a society that is both cissexist and heterosexist, there is a certain degree of privilege accorded to individuals whose appearance and gender expression are read as cisgender, regardless of their personal gender identity. Another example is people who present themselves as heterosexual, regardless of their actual sexual orientation. This privilege is accorded because these heterosexual and cisgender identities are considered "normal", or not transgressing expected and enforced social norms (Bardwell, 2012).

*People have a variety of important reasons for choosing to present as not-queer and, similarly, many others do not have the privilege of this choice (hicks, 2017a).

Coming out: A continual process through which someone recognizes their own sexual orientation or gender identity and is open about it with themselves and with others. It is important to remember that coming out is not something that a person does only once, but rather something that happens over and over again in a variety of situations as they move through a world where heterosexist and cissexist assumptions are constantly being made (Bardwell, 2012).

To "out" someone: To publicly disclose another person's sexual orientation or gender identity without their permission. This is often done without a person's knowledge, is never appropriate, and can also be dangerous for the outed individual.

To be closeted: To be "in the closet" is a pop-culture term used to describe someone who keeps their sexual orientation or gender identity private or secret. People may choose to remain "closeted" for a variety of reasons, including personal safety (Bardwell, 2012). It is still a privilege to live somewhere where you can feel comfortable being "out" and it is therefore important to remember that "closeted" should not be used with a negative or demeaning connotation.

Misgender: When one does not refer to another person using the gendered language that person is most comfortable with. This can be done using any type of gendered language, including words like "man," "woman," "ladies and gentlemen," "girls and boys," or specific gendered pronouns (Bardwell, 2012). Intentional (and/or ongoing apathetic) misgendering is extremely disrespectful and can be hurtful and/or dangerous, especially for trans/GD individuals. For example, if you consistently misgender a person in public spaces you may also be outing them as trans/GD in a place where it is not safe to be read as queer.

Dead naming: This practice is similar to misgendering and involves referring to a trans/GD person by their previous name/name-given-at-birth, even though they have already changed their name to more accurately reflect their identity.

- The term "dead name" is used by some but not all trans/GD people.
- The term is a personal choice and is not for anyone other than that individual to decide whether it feels accurate and appropriate to them.

Section 11: Ending on a FABULOUS Note

Ally: Someone who works to advocate for and support members of a
community that they themselves do not belong to directly. This
support should only be provided on the terms specified by
members of that community, and can take a variety of forms
(Bardwell, 2012). Ultimately it is up to the people who are part
of the group you aim to ally yourself with to decide if you are
indeed an ally.

*It is also important to remember that allyship requires ACTION
(hicks, 2017a).

Intersectionality: This is a feminist sociological concept, which
recognizes that identity is complex and that any individual
may occupy several social identities at the same time (Bardwell,
2012).

*For a more detailed outline of this concept (written in the more
comprehensive context of anti-Black racism + misogynoir + sexism),
please consider watching this TED Talk by Kimberlé Crenshaw:
https://www.ted.com/talks/kimberle_crenshaw_the_urgency_of_inter
sectionality.
   Kimberlé Crenshaw, a professor of law at UCLA and Columbia
Law School, is a leading authority in the area of civil rights, Black
feminist legal theory, race, and racism. Her work has been founda-
tional in two fields of study that have come to be known by terms that
she coined: critical race theory and intersectionality.

Gender neutral washrooms: Washrooms available for use by people of
all genders.

*Also referred to as "all-gender washrooms" or "washrooms for
everyone."
   To conclude, a quote by Cory Silverberg and Fiona Smyth from
their 2015 book, *Sex is a Funny Word*: "Pay close attention to the
words people use when they talk about themselves. Trust yourself to
know what words feel right for you, (and) the one who knows most
about who you are is you."

Some Additional Resources:

The Gender Book – pwyc downloads
http://www.thegenderbook.com/safer-spaces-pack/4583019812

Rainbow Health Ontario – training and education
http://www.rainbowhealthontario.ca/wpcontent/uploads/woocommer
ce_uploads/2015/05/Training-Description.pdf

Family Services Ottawa – around the rainbow
http://familyservicesottawa.org/children-youth-and-families/around-
the-rainbow/

LGBTQ Parenting Network – trans parenting
http://lgbtqpn.ca/transparenting/?doing_wp_cron=1486564285.
6289639472961425781250

Canadian Centre for Gender and Sexual Diversity Studies (CCGSD)
http://ccgsd-ccdgs.org/

EGALE Canadian Human Rights Trust
https://egale.ca/

Intersex Society of North America (ISNA)
http://www.isna.org/

They is My Pronoun
http://theyismypronoun.com/

The No Big Deal Campaign (nbdcampaign)
http://www.nbdcampaign.ca/

- NBD badge and infographics
- http://www.nbdcampaign.ca/shareable-things

Note

1 Pyne, J. (2015). "Discredited treatment of trans kids at CAMH shouldn't
  shock us." *The Toronto Star*, December 17, 2015. https://www.thestar.com/
  opinion/commentary/2015/12/17/discredited-treatment-of-trans-kids-at-
  camh-shouldnt-shock-us.html.

SNAKES AND LADDERS

By Tara Goldstein
Originally written: July, 2004.

Edited: March 2009 for publication in
The International Journal of Critical Pedagogy 3 (1) (2010).

Edited: April 2018 for publication in
Teaching Gender and Sexuality: Letters to Teachers

SNAKES AND LADDERS[1]

Characters (In order of appearance)

Rachel Davis:	Teacher; born in Toronto; White; Jewish; lesbian; cisgender; early 30s.
Karen Diamond:	First-year principal; born in Toronto; White; Anglo-Saxon Protestant; straight; cisgender; early 40s.
Anne James:	Teacher; born in Jamaica; Black; Christian; straight; cisgender; early 40s.
Amy Evans:	Student teacher; born in Toronto; White; Anglo-Saxon Protestant; questioning; cisgender; early 20s.
John Allen:	Student teacher; born in Toronto; White; Anglo-Saxon Protestant; straight; cisgender; late 20s.
Roberto Rodriguez:	Student teacher; born in South America, immigrated to Canada at the age of 12; raised Southern Baptist; gay; cisgender; early 20s.
Rahima Ali:	Student teacher; born in Toronto; Pakistani descent; Muslim; straight; cisgender; early 20s.
Bob Byers:	Experienced principal; born in Toronto; White; Anglo-Saxon Protestant; straight; cisgender; early 50s.

The Gay Straight Alliance (GSA)

Chris:	Student; born in Toronto; White; Anglo-Saxon Protestant; gay; cisgender; 16.

Helen: Student; born in Toronto; Chinese; straight; cisgen-
            der; 16.

Students and Teachers Against Racism (STAR)

Ray: Student; born in Toronto; Caribbean descent; straight; cis-
            gender; 15.
Diane: Student; born in Toronto; Caribbean descent; straight; cis-
            gender; 15.

Flashback scene

Young Roberto: Student; questioning; cisgender; 15.
Roberto's friend: Student; race, ethnicity open; straight; cisgen-
                    der; 15.
Hotline counsellor: Race and ethnicity open; queer; early 20s.
Roberto's father   Born in South America; Southern Baptist;
                    straight; cisgender; late 30s.
Roberto's mother: Born in South America; Southern Baptist;
                    straight; cisgender; mid 30s.

School Council scene

Sara Phillips: Student teacher; born in Toronto; Anglo-Saxon Pro-
                    testant; European descent; lesbian; cisgender; early 20s.
Parent 1:   Race, ethnicity open; straight; cisgender; late 30s.
Parent 2:   Race, ethnicity open; straight; cisgender; late 30s.
Parent 3:   Race, ethnicity open; straight; cisgender; late 30s.

Setting:
Pierre Elliot Trudeau Secondary School
Toronto, Canada
Spring 2003

Scene 1

Principal's office. Rachel's classroom. English office.
RACHEL: *(Sticking her head into the principal's office)* Hi Karen. Did you
    have a chance to read the GSA's proposal for putting on Pride Day?

KAREN: Yes. And I have a lot of questions.

RACHEL: Oh?

KAREN: *(Looking at her watch)* Starting with, what does GSA stand for?

RACHEL: Gay Straight Alliance.

KAREN: We have a student group called Gay Alliance?

RACHEL: Yeah – I mean, no. I mean it's called Gay *Straight* Alliance.

KAREN: Why didn't I know about it?

> *(AMY, ROBERTO, RAHIMA and JOHN enter, walk over to the principal's office, and then wait for KAREN)*

RACHEL: *(Surprised)* Well, uh, I'm not sure. We got started late last year. Before you arrived. We're listed in the Student Agenda book.

KAREN: I didn't see it. *(Looks at her watch)* Rachel, I'm sorry, but I have another meeting in five minutes. We'll have to talk about this later. But I want you to know that I am very surprised to hear that we have a gay group here. *(Pause)* I don't like surprises.

RACHEL: But it's not a gay group. It's a Gay Straight Alliance group. The students talk about discrimination. Homophobia.

KAREN: Who started the group?

RACHEL: One of my students approached me last year and asked me to be the faculty sponsor. Helen Lee. She's Jeffrey Lee's sister. Jeffrey was a gay Grade 11 student who transferred out last year because of verbal harassment.

KAREN: What kind of harassment?

RACHEL: Three of his classmates surrounded him at his locker and taunted him.

KAREN: What did they say?

RACHEL: Things like "Are you gay, guy?" "Are you gay?" "Are you a fag? We think you're a faggot." Karen, those words are just as hurtful as "Paki" or "Chink". And you know how hard we try to make sure that we don't let those slurs go by. If we had had a Gay Straight Alliance group here last year, Jeffrey Lee would have had a place to come and talk about what was happening. Maybe he'd still be here.

KAREN: *(Looks out of her office)* Your student teachers are waiting outside. Look, I appreciate what you're saying. We need to talk about this some more. But Rachel, we're teachers, not social workers. It's not our role to facilitate support groups for gay kids. We're not experts. We have counsellors we can refer students like Jeffrey to if necessary.

RACHEL: But –

KAREN: *(Moves closer to RACHEL, lowers her voice)* Most parents don't want their children to hear about regular sex at school, never mind gay sex. I need to talk to the student teachers. I'll see you tomorrow.

(RACHEL leaves the office, nods at the student teachers and walks to her classroom. KAREN greets the student teachers)

KAREN: Good morning, everyone.

RAHIMA: Good morning.

ROBERTO: Morning.

AMY: Hi.

KAREN: Please come in and have a seat.

(RAHIMA, ROBERTO and AMY enter the office and sit down)

JOHN: *(Enters last, walks over to KAREN and shakes her hand)* Hello, nice to meet you. *(Seeing that there aren't any chairs left)* I'll stand.

KAREN: *(Smiles at JOHN)* So will I. It's John, right?

JOHN: Right.

KAREN: Welcome to Pierre Elliot Trudeau. I hope you all had a good first day yesterday.

(All four nod and smile)

KAREN (CONT'D): I know you are going to have a wonderful experience at Pierre Elliot Trudeau. Anne James and Rachel Davis are both strong teachers and you'll learn a lot from them. The students here are academically inclined. Almost all will go on to university. But, more importantly, we're a friendly school. Everyone gets along.

(All four nod and smile)

KAREN: I want you to know that I have two openings in the English department next year.

(All speaking at the same time)

RAHIMA: Really?

ROBERTO: Wow.

AMY: That's great.

JOHN: That's excellent news.

KAREN: If you like it here, and I'm sure you will, let me know. I prefer hiring teachers who have already taught with us. *(Looks at her watch)* One more thing before I let you go. I know you'll be very busy with your teaching assignments, but I recommend that you all get involved with some extra-curricular activity. There's more to school life than what goes on in the classroom. I need teachers who will work with students outside of class.

(All four nod)

(RAHIMA, ROBERTO, AMY, and JOHN walk back to the English office and sit down)

Scene 2

Principal's office.

KAREN: *(On the phone)* Principal Byers, please. *(Pause)* Thank you. *(Pause)* Hi Bob, it's Karen Diamond from Pierre Elliot Trudeau. How are you? *(Pause)* Good. *(Pause)* Pretty good. Busy. Lots to learn in the first year. And we have 15 student teachers here this semester. Bob, can I run something by you? *(Brief pause)* Thanks. I just found out that one of my teachers is running a Gay Straight Alliance group. And I'm worried. *(Pause)* Well, I don't want to be involved in a huge controversy the first year I'm principal here. There are lots of people watching me. We have some kids from religious families here. *(Pause)* Sorry? *(Pause)* Oh. I guess I'm thinking of the Muslim families. What if some of the parents object? What if they complain to the superintendent? I love this school. I was a teacher here for 10 years before getting my principal papers, and I have been waiting five years for this position to open up. I don't want to be transferred. *(Pause)* No, she's not asking for approval. She got approval to run the group at the end of last year. Don't ask me how. *(Pause)* Oh. I didn't know the new equity policy included anti-homophobia. I thought it was mostly about racism. *(Pause)* It's been running since September. *(Pause)* No, no calls yet. *(Pause)* No. In fact I don't know her at all. She arrived after I took the V-P position at West End Academy. *(Pause)* Drama and English. *(Pause)* Yeah. Very good. The kids like her a lot. *(Pause)* Would you? Thanks a lot. I really appreciate it. I'll see you next week.

Scene 3

The English classroom.

(ANNE enters and sits down near RACHEL)

RACHEL: I tried to explain that it wasn't a gay group and that we were talking about homophobia, not sex. But she couldn't hear me. For her, talking about gay issues means talking about sex. Homosexuals are homo-*sex*-uals.

ANNE: Part of the problem was that she didn't know that there was a GSA at the school.

RACHEL: That's not my fault is it? I mean, the group is in the Student Agenda book.

ANNE: It would have been a good idea to talk to her about the group at the beginning of the year, maybe invite her to a meeting so –

RACHEL: You know, I have a real problem with that. Bill didn't have to go in and talk to her about running the basketball team. And Sandra didn't have to talk to her about the choir, but I have to talk to her about the GSA?

(ANNE shrugs her shoulders)

RACHEL: Did you go in to talk to her about your anti-racism group?

ANNE: Actually, yes I did. I have a friend at West End Academy. She warned me. Karen Diamond hates surprises. And controversy makes her nervous. So in September I made an appointment. I told her about the group, invited her to a STAR meeting, and let her know that we wanted to do something on March 21, the International Day for the Elimination of Racism.

RACHEL: That was smart.

ANNE: So how did you leave things?

RACHEL: She told me that she doesn't think we need a GSA at the school because everyone gets along. That's outrageous. You can't walk down the hall of this school without hearing someone yell out "fag" or "faggot". Most teachers let the slurs and jokes slide. They pretend they didn't hear anything.

(ANNE nods)

RACHEL: And then at lunch, I found a note in my box saying that she wants to come to the next meeting.

ANNE: Really?

RACHEL: The kids think that we are going to be discussing the first Pride Day ever at the school and the principal is coming to the meeting to shut down the group.

ANNE: Well, you don't know that for sure. But I am really sorry to hear all this. *(Pause)* There's a student in my Creative Writing class who I think is wondering about his sexuality. He's also a member of STAR. I wanted to suggest that he go to your next meeting, but hadn't quite figured how to go about it. I mean, if someone hasn't come out to you, and maybe hasn't even come out to himself and you suggest he attend a GSA meeting, it seems intrusive. But I really think he needs to be in a space where he can hear people talk about gay people in a positive way.

RACHEL: You see. That's exactly why holding a school-wide Pride Day is so important. It's a chance for the whole school to hear positive things about gay people. And to do some anti-homophobia education. I can't believe we're going to be shut down.

ANNE: *(Puts her hand on Rachel's arm)* I think I have an idea.

Scene 4

The cafeteria.

(RAHIMA and ROBERTO are standing at the back, supervising lunch)

RAHIMA: Did you have to supervise the cafeteria during your first placement?

ROBERTO: No. You?

RAHIMA: Yeah.

ROBERTO: Every day?

RAHIMA: Every second day.

ROBERTO: Well, that's one way to get to know the kids.

RAHIMA: True. A lot of Pakistani girls came up to talk to me at lunch. They told me that they had never had a Muslim teacher before.

ROBERTO: That must have been cool. Being their first Muslim teacher.

RAHIMA: Very cool. I'd love to get a job there. I'd start up a club for Muslim students.

ROBERTO: To challenge Islamophobia.

RAHIMA: Exactly.

ROBERTO: That was a great workshop your group did in our School and Society class. I've never been to an anti-Islamophobia workshop before. I was kind of surprised at how many misconceptions people had about the Islamic faith and Muslims.

RAHIMA: *(Nods)* There's a lot of work to do. But on a completely different topic, I've been thinking about your grandmother. How's she doing?

ROBERTO: Much better. She's home from the hospital and staying with my parents. Thanks for asking. I'm going to try and visit her this weekend.

RAHIMA: I'm sure she'll be glad to see you. *(Looks at her watch)* That's it. Lunch is over. *(Smiles)* I'll see you later.

ROBERTO: Later.

> *(RAHIMA, ROBERTO, AMY and JOHN all walk to the English classroom. JOHN carries a notebook. Everyone but JOHN sits on the chairs. RACHEL and ANNE lean against the desk. JOHN stands)*

Scene 5

English classroom.

ANNE: As you may already know, March 21 is the International Day to Eliminate Racism. The school's Students and Teachers Against Racism group – STAR – is planning a series of events and I'd like all four of you to be involved.

RAHIMA: I'd love to be involved.

ROBERTO: Me too.

AMY: Sounds great.

ANNE: Rachel and I have been talking. Rachel's the faculty advisor of the Gay Straight Alliance.

ROBERTO: There's a Gay Straight Alliance group at Trudeau?

> *(JOHN takes a pen out of his pocket and starts doodling on his notebook)*

RACHEL: Yes. It started last year.

ANNE: While the two groups have not worked with each other before, we thought it was time to bring them together. Rachel's group has been talking about putting on a Pride Day at Trudeau. We decided that this year, to commemorate our week of working towards eliminating racism and discrimination, we are going to put on a set of Pride Days. Racial and Ethnic Pride, and Gay Pride.

ROBERTO: Wow.

RACHEL: We still have to clear the idea with Karen. And we also need to talk to the students in the GSA and STAR. But we wanted to let you know we're counting on your help. We only have four weeks to get everything organized.

JOHN: I've already told Gary Wilson I'd help him out with the Snakes and Ladders Competition. My second teachable is History.

ROBERTO: What's the Snakes and Ladders Competition?

JOHN: It's a contest sponsored by the History Department. Students answer questions in different categories, like World History, Canadian History, American History. If they are right, they roll the dice and work their way up and down the Snakes and Ladders game board.

RACHEL: It's very popular.

ROBERTO: Maybe we could come up with a special set of questions for each Pride Day. You know, like, special questions on Canadian Black History or Canadian Asian History for Racial Pride and questions on Gay History for Gay –

RACHEL: That's a great idea, Roberto. I'll talk to Gary and see what he says. Any other ideas?

> *(ANNE and RACHEL walk offstage. JOHN and AMY walk to the English office. RAHIMA and ROBERTO stay in the classroom)*

Scene 6

English office.

AMY: How's Marcia doing? Is she still dealing with morning sickness?

JOHN: Yeah. It's still pretty bad.

AMY: When's she due?

JOHN: Sometime in August. We're hoping that she'll be able to go on maternity leave for a full year. I guess it will depend on whether or not I have a teaching job in September.

AMY: Maybe you'll get a job here. You're certainly making a good impression. You work every lunch hour running the Snakes and Ladders game. And you're here until 5 or 6 every night marking and preparing questions.

JOHN: I'd love to get a job here. I really hope all this pays off. I had to change my tutoring appointments to stay after school, so I'm working on both Saturday and Sunday now.

AMY: Sounds like you're really busy.

JOHN: Yeah.

AMY: Are you too busy to come for a drink at the Duke next Friday? Sara's trying to get everyone in the cohort together. She asked me to invite everyone here.

JOHN: Thanks, but I'm going to be tutoring.

AMY: Too bad. It's going to be a good time. People are going to let off a little steam.

JOHN: *(Grinning)* Well, if Sara's organizing it, it will be a party.

AMY: *(Grinning back)* Yeah.

JOHN: I don't have to ask if you'll be going.

AMY: *(Laughing)* No.

JOHN: You two are as close as peas in a pod.

AMY: *(Startled)* What do you mean?

JOHN: Nothing. Just that you two are always together. You see one, you see the other.

    (AMY is silent)

    (Changes the subject) So how's Sara's practice teaching going?

AMY: Fine. But she'd rather be here and working on Pride Days.

JOHN: *(Nodding)* Yeah. She'd be right in the middle of Pride Days. *(Looks at his watch)* Well, gotta go. Say hi to Sara when you see her. And have a beer for me.

Scene 7

English classroom.

ROBERTO: Has Amy told you about the get-together next Friday?

RAHIMA: Yeah. Are you going to go?

ROBERTO: I think so. You?

RAHIMA: It's at a bar. I don't go to events where they serve alcohol.

ROBERTO: I didn't know that. *(Pause)* Is that why you didn't go to the other party before practice teaching?

RAHIMA: Partly. I mean, I had a family event that night, as well. But if they hadn't served alcohol I probably would have come, at least for a while.

ROBERTO: Maybe you should email Sara. She could plan something else.

RAHIMA: It's always awkward. There are only two of us who don't go to events where there's alcohol. People think we're extreme.

ROBERTO: Extreme?

RAHIMA: They respect our choice not to drink, but can't understand why we won't attend a social event where there's drinking.

ROBERTO: I think Sara would understand.

RAHIMA: I don't know. People don't like to change the way they usually do something.

ROBERTO: Maybe. But I still think you should talk to Sara.

    (RACHEL enters)

RAHIMA: Hi. How's it going?

ROBERTO AND RAHIMA: Fine.

ROBERTO: I've finished marking all the papers you gave me.

RACHEL: Thanks so much. I really appreciate it.

RAHIMA: *(Looks at her watch)* I've gotta go and set up for my next class. See you later.

ROBERTO: Later.

RACHEL: Have a good class.

RAHIMA: Thanks.

    (RAHIMA exits)

ROBERTO: Rachel, can I ask you about something?

RACHEL: Sure.

ROBERTO: I came in early this morning to get my photocopying done for first period, and I ran into one of the V-Ps in the parking lot.

RACHEL: Which one?

ROBERTO: Brian Hanson. He noticed the rainbow sticker on my car. *(Speaking quickly)* You know, I had thought about it. Should I take the car to school? Should I park it in the lot? Should I take the subway? But I had all this stuff to take today so I decided to just drive in.

RACHEL: What did he say?

ROBERTO: He looked at the sticker, then he looked at me and said, "You know, if you want to get around having any reaction, you can just back the car in." It's not like I had asked him about the sticker on the car. He just noticed it and decided I should back it in. Has anything like that happened to you?

RACHEL: No. I don't have a rainbow sticker on the back of my car.

ROBERTO: It's so disappointing. On one hand, the school has a Gay Straight Alliance and is planning a Gay Pride Day and, on the other, Brian advises me to back my car into a parking spot so that people won't think I'm gay.

RACHEL: You need to remember that we haven't been given permission to hold Pride Day yet. And the GSA is only a year old. We've only begun to do the anti-homophobia work we need to do here. Brian worries about teachers being out at school so –

ROBERTO: What's he so worried about? You're out, aren't you?

RACHEL: Yes. But not everyone thinks it's a good idea. You know, there are still lots of parents who don't like the idea of gay and lesbian teachers in their kids' school.

ROBERTO: That's –

RACHEL: I know, I know. I'm just saying that lots of parents are uncomfortable. They don't know any gay people themselves and –

ROBERTO: They don't think they know any gay people. But they do. It's just that so many gay people are closeted, that people don't know that they know gay people.

(RACHEL is silent)

Sorry, I interrupted you.

RACHEL: No, that's okay. I agree with you. It's just that there's still a myth out there … I mean, people – some people – believe that gay men and lesbians are promiscuous and will try to recruit their children into a gay lifestyle.

ROBERTO: I hate that word.

RACHEL: Promiscuous?

ROBERTO: Lifestyle. I don't have a lifestyle. I have a life.

Scene 8

Principal's office.

KAREN: Thanks for visiting Bob. It's nice to have you here.

BOB: Thanks for showing me around. Your new computer lab is very impressive.

KAREN: We're thrilled to have it.

BOB: I bet. *(Pause)* So what's happened to that Gay Straight Alliance group you were talking about?

KAREN: I think they've joined forces with the anti-racism group.

BOB: Really? Good for them.

KAREN: You think so?

BOB: Yeah. I do. The more school support there is for anti-homophobia work, the better it will be received.

KAREN: Or the more support there is, the bigger the backlash.

> *(BOB smiles)*
>
> Why aren't you worried about the backlash at your school?

BOB: Well, I've been a principal longer than you have. And I've survived more than one conflict in my career. But I guess it's because, for me, the work is personal.

> *(KAREN is silent)*
>
> My daughter is gay. She came out to us in her first year of university.

KAREN: Oh.

BOB: But she had known for quite a while before that.

KAREN: Were you surprised?

BOB: Shocked.

KAREN: Did she have a hard time at school?

BOB: No. Well, not that I know of, anyway. But maybe that's because she was in the closet all through high school.

> *(KAREN is silent)*
>
> You know, when your child comes out, you go into the closet.

KAREN: What do you mean?

BOB: After she told us, when people asked about Shannon, I wouldn't say anything. I was scared to tell anyone. Even close friends. I was afraid of what they might say to me.

> *(KAREN is silent)*
>
> I was also afraid for her safety. Would she get harassed? Would people call her ugly names? But I couldn't talk about it. I couldn't reach out. A few weeks later I was asked to go to a PD session on the board's new equity policy. When they talked about the five new equity implementation documents and told us that one of them was about challenging homophobia, I felt grateful. Really grateful. I wanted every school, every university to have a document like that so that my daughter and kids like her would be safe. After the session I talked to one of the equity people about Shannon. That was the first time I came out about having a daughter who is lesbian.

KAREN: *(Quietly)* Wow.

BOB: But in order for the policy to do any good, we have to implement it. Even when it's difficult. Even when it brings us into conflict with staff and parents. Karen, the policy needs to be implemented. I'll support you.

(BOB exits. ANNE, AMY, RAHIMA, and students from the GSA and STAR clubs walk to the English classroom carrying enough chairs for almost everyone. People either sit on the seats, or on the desk, or lean up against the desk. The GSA and STAR students sit in two separate groups)

Scene 9

Principal's office. English classroom.

(In the principal's office, KAREN is reading the equity policy. In the classroom, people are talking amongst themselves in their two separate groups. RAHIMA sits with the STAR students, AMY sits next to RAHIMA and ROBERTO walks back and forth between both groups)

RACHEL: *(Looks at her watch, then raises her voice to be heard above the conversation)* Okay. It's getting late. *(People quiet down)* Principal Diamond must be held up. Let's begin without her. Thank you all for coming. The purpose of this meeting is to get your feedback on an idea Ms. James and I have worked on together. Ms. James, would you like to present our proposal?

(KAREN checks her watch, puts down the policy, and hurries towards the English classroom. As she reaches the door she slows down and, instead of entering, stands at the door and listens to the discussion)

ANNE: As the students who participate in STAR know, every year the club puts on a week of events to commemorate March 21, the International Day for Eliminating Racism. This year Ms. Davis and I thought about planning a whole week of events that not only challenge racism, but other forms of discrimination as well. The Gay Straight Alliance has been working on the issue of homophobia and has put together a proposal for a Gay Pride Day.

CHRIS: We're here, we're queer, get used to it!

(The GSA students laugh. The STAR students look uncomfortable)

ANNE: *(Smiling slightly)* What we propose is a set of Pride Days: Racial Pride, Ethnic Pride and Gay Pride.

CHRIS: Why are we calling it Gay Pride? Shouldn't we call it LGBTQ Pride?

RAY: What do all those letters mean?

CHRIS: Lesbian, gay, bisexual, transgender, queer.

HELEN: I thought the "Q" stood for "questioning".

DIANE: What's transgender?

CHRIS: It's used to describe people who live in the gender that is not the one they were raised in. Like a person who was born male and is living as a female or vice versa.

DIANE: Oh.

RAY: Why do we have to have Gay Pride Day during Anti-Racism Week?

DIANE: Yeah. Why don't they celebrate it sometime in June when other gay people celebrate it? March 21 is supposed to be about racism.

ROBERTO: Some people experience racism *and* homophobia. We need to fight both together.

DIANE: *(Matter of fact)* Black people aren't faggots.

HELEN: *(Angry)* What?

RACHEL: *(Calm)* Okay. Hold it there. *(To DIANE)* The last word you used. What was it?

DIANE: *(Embarrassed)* What? Faggots?

RACHEL: Right. How is faggot used in the hallway? Is it a compliment?

HELEN: No.

DIANE: It's not a put down.

RACHEL: Although some people might use it as a joke, I think the consensus is that it's usually used as a put down. So we won't use it. Okay?

DIANE: Okay.

RACHEL: Okay. Before we continue with the proposal, let's talk about the idea that Black people aren't lesbian and gay. Is that true?

RAY: On television the only people who are gay are White.

HELEN: Gay people aren't only White. My brother is Chinese and he's gay. He went to this school last year but had to leave because he was harassed for being a "faggot".

CHRIS: And there's that Sri Lankan guy. The one who wrote that book. What's it called?

AMY: *Funny Boy?*

CHRIS: Yeah.

AMY: Shyam Selvadurai.

CHRIS: Yeah.

ANNE: And Frida Kahlo.

CHRIS: Who's she?

ANNE: A Mexican painter who was famous for her self-portraits. There was a movie done about her recently. It starred Salma Hayek.

HELEN: I loved that movie. But Frida wasn't a lesbian. She was married to that guy, what's his name?

ANNE: Diego Rivera. Kahlo was bisexual. She was married to Rivera, but was also attracted to women.

DIANE: If we help out with Gay Day, people might think that we're gay.

HELEN: I'm going to help out and I'm not gay.

DIANE: But some people may think you are.

CHRIS: What's wrong with people thinking that you're gay?

(DIANE is silent. There's an awkward pause)

ANNE: Mr. Rodriguez, why don't you tell us the ideas you and Ms. Davis have come up with for Gay Pride Day.

CHRIS: We should call it LGBTQ Pride Day.

ANNE: Let's hear from Mr. Rodriguez first. We'll talk about the name after.

ROBERTO: Okay. We talked about inviting a group called T.E.A.C.H. to come and do an anti-homophobia workshop with us. T.E.A.C.H. stands for Teens Educating and Confronting Homophobia. The members of T.E.A.C.H. identify as LGBTQ and straight.

HELEN: Are they all White?

ROBERTO: No. The group is mixed. And as part of the workshop they tell their coming-out stories. The story of when they first knew they might not be or weren't heterosexual. We also thought about holding a special game of Snakes and Ladders on Canadian minority history.

CHRIS: What about a queer talent night? And a drag contest?

DIANE: What's drag?

HELEN: It's when guys dress up like girls and girls dress up like guys.

CHRIS: Or maybe we could put on an "Ask Dr. Ruth" show with questions and answers about queer sex.

KAREN: *(Loud)* Good afternoon everyone.

(People are startled)

I'm sorry I'm late.

(ROBERTO gets up off his seat to provide a seat for KAREN)

Thank you Roberto.

ROBERTO: You're welcome.

KAREN: *(Looks around the room, at each member of the group)* Ms. Davis and Ms. James have talked to me about the idea of Anti-Racism and Pride Week and I've been listening to the last part of your discussion. I have some thoughts. *(To Roberto)* First, I think Mr. Rodriguez makes a good point that some people experience both racism and homophobia and that it is helpful to educate people about both forms of discrimination. That's also what the board equity policy says. So, you have my support for a set of different Pride Days that teaches about tolerance for others.

RACHEL: It's not really about toler–

ANNE: Thank you Karen.

KAREN: *(To RACHEL)* Ms. James and the STAR group have a lot of experience conducting anti-racist education and I am sure that this experience will be helpful to the GSA. But I am concerned about some of the ideas I have heard you talk about. I read the board's pamphlet on "What Anti-Homophobia Education Is and What It Isn't". *(To CHRIS)* The board is clear that anti-homophobia education is *not* sex education. So, there will be no question and answer show about sex.

CHRIS: But –

KAREN: Which brings me to another concern, which is about language. Lots of people don't like that word you used.

CHRIS: Which word?

KAREN: Queer. It makes them uncomfortable. So, I suggest, insist really, you not use it. Since there is some confusion about the term LG – B – QT – GLTB – you know what I mean – and the term transgender, I also suggest you stick with the name Gay Pride Day.

CHRIS: But not all queers are gay. Some are bi, some are –

KAREN: People will understand that you are using the word "Gay" to mean all people who are not heterosexual. Finally, *(looks directly at RAHIMA)* given the religious diversity present in this school, we need to be careful not to offend anyone. This is a school, not a nightclub. So no gay talent night and no drag contest. The T. E.A.C.H. workshop is approved by the board so it's fine. You can contact someone at the board's Equity Office for a list of other resources. *(Looks at her watch, stands up to leave)* I'm sorry, but I have to go. Good luck in your planning. Keep me informed of your progress. I want to see the final program for the entire week.

ANNE: No problem. Thanks for your time.

KAREN: You're welcome. Have a good evening.

ANNE: You too.

(KAREN exits)

CHRIS: If the school is not a nightclub, how come we have straight Talent Night?

(The students and ANNE and RACHEL leave the stage taking the extra chairs with them. RACHEL, ROBERTO and CHRIS remain in the English classroom. AMY and RAHIMA join JOHN in the English office)

Scene 10

English office. The hallway. The English classroom.

(In the English office)

RAHIMA: And then she looks right at me and starts talking about respecting religious diversity at the school. I felt so singled out.

JOHN: But doesn't the Koran say that homosexuality is a sin?

RAHIMA: Yes, but so does the Old Testament. So does the New Testament. Why only look at me when talking about religious objections to homosexuality?

JOHN: Your religious beliefs are visible. Most people's are not.[2]

(RAHIMA and AMY are silent)

AMY: Anyway, by the end of the meeting we all had a long list of things to do. Do you have any time to help me come up with a set of questions for the Pride Day game of Snakes and Ladders?

JOHN: Sorry, I can't. I've got my hands full with the normal Snakes and Ladders game. The finals begin next week, and I just don't have the time.

(ANNE and DIANE enter and stand in the hallway)

ANNE: So what's the problem?

DIANE: I don't want to introduce the people from T.E.A.C.H.

ANNE: Why not?

DIANE: People will think *I'm* gay.

ANNE: In your introduction you can tell people that you are a member of STAR who is there as a straight ally to fight homophobia. If you want, I can get you a button that says "Straight, but not narrow." That way everyone will know you aren't gay.

DIANE: But what if I don't want to be a straight ally?

ANNE: What's the problem with being an ally?

DIANE: It means that I agree that it's okay.

ANNE: That what's okay?

DIANE: That *(looks down at the floor)* it's okay to be a fag- to be gay.

ANNE: I think what we're saying, as straight allies, is that we should all respect other people's differences.

DIANE: But if I don't agree that it's okay to be gay, then shouldn't my opinion be respected?

ANNE: *(Pauses)* I want you to think about something. People are. We have to respect the right of all of us to just be. Be who we are. And that's not easy. And it doesn't happen without some kind of conflict. Because we don't live in the world all by ourselves.

(In the English classroom)

RACHEL: So what's the problem?

CHRIS: It's just not fair.

RACHEL: What's not fair?

CHRIS: That Ms. Diamond gets to say what can and can't happen at Pride Days.

RACHEL: She's the principal.

CHRIS: I know. But can't we, like, protest or something? Can't you talk to her about the drag contest?

RACHEL: What do you want me to say?

CHRIS: Tell her that if the school can host a gospel choir and draw from Black culture to educate about racism, then it's only fair that we host a drag contest and draw from gay culture to educate about homophobia.

(In the English office)

JOHN: So what else are you guys doing for Pride Day?

AMY: Well, I am supposed to facilitate a follow-up discussion on a film that deals with homophobia.

JOHN: That's not too time-consuming. Though I guess you have to preview the film.

AMY: I already have. It's a good film, but I'm very nervous. What happens if someone asks a question or makes a comment and I say the wrong thing?

RAHIMA: Have you talked to Rachel about it?

AMY: Yeah. And she said if I waited until I knew absolutely everything about every topic I was asked to teach I would never teach anything.

JOHN: She has a point.

AMY: Maybe. But that doesn't change how I feel. I'm thinking of asking Roberto to co-facilitate the discussion with me.

RAHIMA: That's a good idea.

JOHN: *(To RAHIMA)* What do you have to do?

RAHIMA: I'm doing a workshop on stereotyping Muslims with a student from STAR. I'm also supposed to organize the visit from T.E.A.C.H. and welcome the speakers.

JOHN: The workshop will take some work, but organizing the visit isn't too hard.

RAHIMA: It's not hard, but it's a problem.

AMY: Why?

RAHIMA: If I welcome the speakers to the school, to Gay Pride Day, it will look like I think it's okay to be gay.

AMY: And you don't.

RAHIMA: No. I mean, I don't believe that gay people should be discriminated against. I bust kids for saying "fag" in the hallway. And I have gay friends in the cohort. Like Roberto. But I don't think it's okay to be gay. You can't be gay and Muslim.

    (ANNE and SHERRY exit downstage left. RACHEL and CHRIS exit. RAHIMA walks to the English classroom and sits down next to ROBERTO)

Scene 11

The English classroom.

ROBERTO: It's not true, you know. You can be gay and Muslim.

RAHIMA: What?

ROBERTO: I have a friend who is Muslim and he's gay. He found this organization on the net. An organization of Muslim gay men. It's called "Al-Fathiha."

    (RAHIMA nods)

    Yeah. It's a group that is working out how to be gay and still follow the faith. *(Pauses, waiting to see if she will say anything)*

    (RAHIMA is silent)

But if you don't want to introduce the T.E.A.C.H. speakers,
I'll do it for you.

RAHIMA: Thank you.

ROBERTO: You're welcome. But in return I want you to co-facilitate the
workshop on name-calling with me.

RAHIMA: Sure.

ROBERTO: I'm planning to look at both racist and homophobic name-
calling.

RAHIMA: Okay.

ROBERTO: Okay.

RAHIMA: Thanks for understanding.

ROBERTO: Yeah. I know what it's like. My family is very religious.

RAHIMA: Really?

ROBERTO: They're members of one of the few congregations of Spanish-
speaking Southern Baptists. To Baptists, homosexuality is a horrible
sin, right up there with killing your father and blaspheming God.

RAHIMA: So I guess you're not out to your family.

ROBERTO: Oh, I'm out.

RAHIMA: You are?

ROBERTO: I've been out since 16.

RAHIMA: Sixteen!

*(YOUNG ROBERTO, ROBERTO'S FRIEND, THE HOT-
LINE COUNSELLOR, ROBERTO'S FATHER and ROBERTO'S
MOTHER enter)*

ROBERTO: People always ask me "When?" "When did you know?" I never
could really pinpoint the exact moment when I knew for sure. But I can
remember the moment that got it all started. I was at a friend's house. I
was in Grade 9 and living in Mississauga. We were looking at the
yearbook and trying to decide who we'd go out with. He had chosen
two or three potential girlfriends or girls at school he'd like to have sex
with. When it came to my turn to choose, we went through the whole
yearbook looking for someone for me to go out with, or at least to do *it*
with me. For every girl in my class, I had some sort of excuse.

YOUNG ROBERTO: She's not my type. She's like a sister to me. I like her,
but not *that* way.

ROBERTO: Then we moved on to girls in other Grade 9 classes. Then to
girls in Grade 10, Grade 11, and Grade 12. After exhausting all the
possibilities, my friend turned to me and said . . .

ROBERTO'S FRIEND: So, we've looked at all the girls in our school, and you haven't chosen any of them. *(In a mocking way)* Would you go out with any guys?

ROBERTO: I was kind of disgusted and kind of insulted.

YOUNG ROBERTO: No. That's gross! A guy? Ugh! Never! That's just too gross to imagine! I guess I'm just not ready to go out with anybody right now.

ROBERTO: And we left it at that. But that got me thinking.

YOUNG ROBERTO: Do I really like boys? I think they're attractive. But doesn't everyone think guys are attractive? I mean, girls look at other girls and think: "Oh, she's so pretty!" "She has great skin!" "She has beautiful hair." "I HATE HER!"

ROBERTO: I thought guys looked at each other and thought the same thing, only that we couldn't say anything because we're supposed to be macho. But was I really attracted to guys as opposed to girls? Why hadn't I ever had any desire to go out with a girl? I mean, I loved girls, but I'd just want to be friends with them. But with guys, I wanted to have a more intimate relationship. I was confused. And horrified! I didn't know much about homosexuality. Just the things that people talked about under their breath and the things kids made fun of in the playground. But I did remember what my parents had said about homosexuals when we had the sex talk. They were the men that we wanted to stay away from because they molested little kids. That's pretty much all I knew about homosexuality, and the fact that it was a perversion and a sin. So there I was with these feelings of abnormality. I didn't know what to do. I thought I was the only person in Mississauga with this problem and I felt really alone. I needed to find some help. The most obvious place to look in was in the phone book. I looked at the white pages under "Gay." I was so relieved to find out that there were so many people with the last name "Gay."

(RAHIMA laughs)

I thought, "Hey I'm not so alone after all!" There was the Gay-Lea dairy company, which made perfect sense to me, since they also produced "homo" milk.

(RAHIMA laughs)

Then I finally found the Lesbian, Gay, Bisexual Youth-Line. I decided to call.

YOUNG ROBERTO: Hello. I'm 15 years old, I live in Mississauga, I think I'm gay, and I don't know what to do.

HOTLINE COUNSELLOR: Okay, do not commit suicide.

RAHIMA: She didn't say that, did she?

ROBERTO: No. I was joking. She referred me to this gay youth support group running out of the 519 Community Centre in downtown Toronto. They met every Tuesday evening and Saturday afternoon. Since it took me two hours to get to downtown Toronto from where I lived, I decided to go on a Saturday. When I got up the courage to go, I told my parents I was going to the library to prepare for a project. I thought there would be at least four other people. I was the one person from Mississauga, then there would be another one from Scarborough, one from Etobicoke, one from downtown and one from North York. I remember wondering if they would all be wearing feather boas and sequin gowns with high heels. Was I dressed up enough for the occasion?

  (RAHIMA laughs)

  But when I got there, there were about 15 or 20 people, and they didn't look like "freaks" at all, but "normal," like me. Whatever that means.

RAHIMA: What did you talk about?

ROBERTO: We talked about coming out, about telling our families, about our school life, about life in Toronto and being gay. They told me about safe sex and gave me a lot of pamphlets with information on using condoms and safe sex. It was exciting. After the meeting a group of us decided to go out for coffee and talk some more. Then they invited me to play pool. Then we went to another person's house to see a movie. Well, before I knew it, it was 11 o'clock at night. I freaked out and raced to the subway station in order to catch the bus to Mississauga. I got to my house two hours later, at like 1 in the morning.

RAHIMA: Oh, no.

ROBERTO: When I walked in the door, my mom was crying and my dad was calling the police.

ROBERTO'S FATHER: Where have you been?

YOUNG ROBERTO: At the library and afterwards I went to a friend's house.

ROBERTO'S FATHER: Which friend?

YOUNG ROBERTO: Uhm, Chris.

ROBERTO'S FATHER: We called your friend Chris. We called all your friends and everyone from Church. Where have you been?

YOUNG ROBERTO: I was in downtown Toronto.

(Roberto's parents gasp)

ROBERTO: For my South American, Southern Baptist, conservative parents who lived in Mississauga, downtown Toronto was like the dark pit of hell.

ROBERTO'S MOTHER: What were you doing in downtown Toronto? Are you doing drugs?

YOUNG ROBERTO: No, no, it's none of that!

ROBERTO'S MOTHER: Then tell us! We're your parents, we love you, and we want to know what's going on.

YOUNG ROBERTO: I'm sorry I can't. *(Pause)* I can't tell you what I was doing downtown. All I can ask you to do is pray for me.

ROBERTO: We talked for a bit longer in my room. We cried, we prayed. I'll spare you the mushy details. It was late. Finally, we went to sleep. The next morning my parents came into my room and woke me up very softly.

ROBERTO'S MOTHER: *(Whispers)* Robby, wake up.

YOUNG ROBERTO: *(Sleepy)* Wha – what's going on?

ROBERTO'S MOTHER: We want to talk to you for a second.

YOUNG ROBERTO: *(Sleepy)* What?

ROBERTO'S MOTHER: We think we know what's wrong with you.

YOUNG ROBERTO: *(Still sleepy)* What?

ROBERTO'S MOTHER: We think we *know* what's wrong with you.

YOUNG ROBERTO: *(Suddenly wide awake)* You think you know?

ROBERTO'S MOTHER: *(Calm)* Yes, we think we know.

YOUNG ROBERTO: How?

ROBERTO'S FATHER: We found these in your bag.

RAHIMA: What? What did they find?

ROBERTO: The pamphlets and flyers I had received at the meeting. I went pale. I could feel the blood draining from my head. I couldn't breathe. My mother was holding a pamphlet showing a man putting a condom on another man's penis.

RAHIMA: Oh, no.

ROBERTO: My dad was holding a pamphlet talking about the use of dental dams and rimming. *(Pause)* I was mortified.

ROBERTO'S MOTHER: *(Calm)* It's okay. You're our son and we love you. We know that with God's help you will change.

ROBERTO: So that's how I came out to my parents.

RAHIMA: And you never changed.

ROBERTO: I never changed. But because I came out when I was 16, I've had plenty of time to work it out with my parents.

RAHIMA: Do you still go to church?

ROBERTO: No. But I know other gay people who do. Some of them go to the Metropolitan Community Church, downtown. Others go to welcoming United and Anglican churches. These folks, they're Christian and gay.

> *(YOUNG ROBERTO, ROBERTO'S FRIEND, THE HOT-LINE COUNSELLOR, ROBERTO'S FATHER and ROBERTO'S MOTHER exit) ROBERTO AND RAHIMA walk to the English office. KAREN, ANNE, RACHEL enter and sit down in the principal's office)*

Scene 12

Principal's office.

RACHEL: We put them up yesterday afternoon, after school. Fifty of them. Then we checked on them at lunch. Ten had been torn down or defaced.

KAREN: Defaced how?

RACHEL: With graffiti. Next to the word homophobia, one said "We're not afraid, we just don't agree." There was another that said "God hates fags."

KAREN: I assume that –

RACHEL: We took down the posters that had been defaced.

ANNE: This is all very disturbing. In the last few years that STAR has put on Anti-Racism Week, there's been low attendance at some workshops, hot discussions in others, some resistance from teachers. But none of our posters has been defaced in this way.

KAREN: So what's next?

RACHEL: We need to send a strong message that this will not be tolerated. That students caught tearing down or defacing the posters will be suspended. And I think you need to tell students this face-to-face. In an assembly. Tomorrow morning.

KAREN: Can it wait? I have an important meeting tomorrow morning.

ANNE: I don't think we should wait.

KAREN: *(Sighs)* Okay. We schedule the assembly for first period.

RACHEL: Karen, I'm sorry about this.

ANNE: It's not your fault. *(Pause)* In fact, it proves your point. There's work to be done in our school.

>   *(ANNE and RACHEL walk to the English classroom. ROBERTO, AMY, RAHIMA, and students from the GSA and STAR clubs walk to the English classroom carrying enough chairs for almost everyone. People either sit on the seats or on the desk or lean up against the desk. The GSA and STAR students sit in two separate groups)*

Scene 13

The English classroom.

RACHEL: Spring break begins next week, so this is our last meeting before Anti-Racism and Pride Week. I want to talk about any outstanding issues and confirm who's doing what when. Okay. Outstanding issues.

>   *(Everyone is silent)*
>   No outstanding issues?

CHRIS: Did they find the people who were tearing down and writing on the posters?

RACHEL: No. But after the assembly there were no more incidents.

HELEN: Lots of people are saying that they won't be going to the anti-homophobia workshops.

RACHEL: Four teachers are taking their entire classes to the T.E.A.C.H. workshops on Thursday morning. And if there are less people at the lunchtime workshops, so what?

ANNE: We'll work with who shows up.

RAY: We had more anti-racist workshops last year.

ANNE: We did. But we agreed to try something different this year. We'll evaluate what happens and decide what changes we want to make next year.

CHRIS: Well, at least you get to have your gospel choir perform. Ms. Diamond won't let us have a drag contest.

RAY: You can't compare a drag contest to a gospel choir.

CHRIS: Yes, you can. If you take queer culture seriously.

RACHEL: I know you're disappointed about the drag contest, but we agreed that presenting the workshops and films Ms. Diamond approved of was a way to begin.

ROBERTO: We also agreed that we would try not to pitch the anti-racist work against the anti-homophobia work and vice-versa.

CHRIS: I know, but –

KAREN'S VOICE ON THE INTERCOM: Please excuse the interruption. Are Ms. Davis and Ms. James there?

(RAHIMA, who is sitting close to the intercom, catches ANNE's eye. ANNE nods)

RAHIMA: *(Turns on and speaks into the intercom)* Yes.

KAREN'S VOICE ON THE INTERCOM: Could you ask them both to come to my office? I need to speak to them immediately.

(ANNE and RACHEL get up to leave the classroom)

RAHIMA: They're on their way.

ANNE: Ms. Ali, would you go over who's doing what when? If we're not back by the time you've finished that, you can close the meeting.

RAHIMA: Okay.

(ANNE and RACHEL walk over and enter the principal's office)

ANNE: What's up?

KAREN: One of our parents has called the superintendent to complain about Anti-Racism and Pride Week.

RACHEL: What?

ANNE: What's the problem?

KAREN: He doesn't want the topic of homophobia discussed in school.

RACHEL: Why?

KAREN: He says *(looks at the notes she made)* talking about homophobia is a vehicle to promote homosexuality. And *(embarrassed)* he says that homosexuality is not a normal lifestyle.

ANNE: Did you tell the superintendent that our workshops are about condemning homophobic violence and creating safe schools, not promoting homosexuality?

KAREN: Yes. And I reminded him of the board's equity policy.

ANNE: And?

KAREN: He told the parent that he should attend our next School Council meeting and raise his concern there.

RACHEL: But Anti-Racism and Pride Week begins on the Monday after spring break. When's the next School Council meeting?

KAREN: Tuesday of that week.

ANNE: Is Anti-Racism and Pride Week in jeopardy?

KAREN: I don't know.

ANNE: We've all worked so hard. The work is so important. If any of the activities are cancelled, the kids will be very upset.

RACHEL: Only one call. One call from one parent. In a school of almost 1,200 students.

KAREN: What we don't know is how many other concerned parents might show up at the meeting. We'll just have to wait and see.

RACHEL: What about the stuff we planned for Monday and Tuesday? Before the School Council meeting?

ANNE: I think it would be good to go ahead with what we've planned. If there's a lot of pressure to cancel the anti-homophobia workshops, at least we'll have done a little work.

RACHEL: Most of the anti-homophobia stuff is planned for Wednesday and Thursday. T.E.A.C.H. doesn't come until Thursday. *(Pause)* I can't believe this is happening.

ANNE: *(Puts her arm around RACHEL's shoulder)* Don't worry. We'll help the kids prepare a response to the concerns that might be raised. It will be a lesson in struggle. Our kids will learn we can't take our human rights for granted.

Scene 14

The School Council meeting.

AMY: *(Looks at her watch)* It's almost 8. It'll start in a few minutes. Sara, thanks again for coming.

SARA: *(Puts her hand on Amy's arm)* My pleasure. I'm happy to support you. Where's John?

AMY: He's standing at the back. Near the window.

SARA: Right. I see him. Hey, do you want to go out for beer after we're done? Just one, it's a school night.

AMY: I'd love to.

SARA: Great.

AMY: *(Tentative)* There's something I want to talk to you about.

SARA: We'll catch up.

KAREN: *(Looks at her watch)* Good evening everyone. It's now 8 o'clock. Let's begin. There are several items on tonight's agenda. We're going to begin with a discussion on Anti-Racism and Pride Week so that those of you who are here for this particular discussion can leave as soon as it's done. *(Takes a deep breath)* Two of our faculty, Rachel Davis and Anne James, have prepared a list of the activities taking place this week at Pierre Elliot Trudeau. That list is being circulated. Ms. Davis has also copied the board's Equity Foundation Statement for you to read. All of our activities this week are an attempt to implement the board's equity policy. *(Pauses)* The floor is open for questions and comments.

PARENT 1: I am a parent with two kids in this school. I don't want my kids learning about homosexuality from gay and lesbian guest speakers who have been invited to the school to share their coming-out stories. Our church teaches that homosexuality is wrong. We do not believe it's a normal lifestyle. It is not the school's place to contradict what we teach our children at home.

PARENT 2: Even if you don't believe in the gay lifestyle, and you feel that this is against your religion and not a good thing and against God. Don't you think it's helpful that the school opens the topic so that you can teach what you believe to your child? It's hard to talk about this. So when our kids come home with questions, it opens the dialogue. Even if you are against *(makes imaginary quotation marks with her hands)* "the lifestyle," don't you think it still needs to be addressed?

PARENT 1: Not by the school.

ANNE: My church also taught me that to be gay or lesbian was wrong. And I brought that with me because I don't stop being Christian when I walk into the building. So I have had to work really hard coming to terms with what I've been taught. Because I know that in my classroom, at my school, I have to be there for all my students. I have to affirm who they are and that includes kids of gay and lesbian families and kids who may be gay or lesbian themselves. I know what it's like not to be affirmed at school. I want my students' school experience to be different.

PARENT 3: I agree that we shouldn't throw stones. But I don't believe that we should be using taxpayers' money for promoting homosexuality either. It's up to parents to teach their children about sexuality, according to their own set of moral values.

PARENT 1: I agree.

RACHEL: It's not appropriate that values only be taught at home. There are social values, community values. When teachers allow one student to hurl the word "faggot" at another and don't address the issue, I think it's unconscionable. What message does the student get? The student gets the message that it's okay to verbally assault gay people. If it weren't, then the teacher would step in. And what happens when the student who was called a "faggot" suspects they're gay and needs to talk to someone about it. He thinks I can't let anyone know. They'll think there's something wrong with me. Because when I was called a "faggot" last year, they thought it was okay.

HELEN: My brother Jeffrey used to be a student at this school. And when he was in Grade 9 he was called a "faggot" almost every day. When he finally told me what was going on I tried to help him. But there wasn't anything that I could do on my own. Jeffrey finally got so depressed that he refused to go to school. That's when my parents decided to transfer him to another school.

RAHIMA: What Helen has just said is very important. We need to stop the name-calling that goes on in our school. Many of the events that have been planned for Anti-Racism and Pride Week have been designed to help us do that.

CHRIS: Homophobia is not only about name-calling. It's also about being beat up.

ROBERTO: In addition to the issue of gay bashing, there's the issue of suicide. The amount of suicides and attempted suicides by gay, lesbian, and questioning youth is alarming. Thirty percent of all youth suicides are undertaken by gay and lesbian youth. Because our society is saying it's not okay to be gay, kids think that *they* aren't okay. So what do they do? They try to kill themselves. We are not taking good care of our kids.

SARA: When I was growing up, nobody ever gave me any sense that it was okay to be who I was – a lesbian – or that there was support, resources for me, anything. I want to help the students I teach to grow up knowing, grow up feeling it's okay and not to feel so isolated. At some churches they believe that there is God in every person and those people include queer people too.

PARENT 1: That's fine for people who attend those churches, but not for me. All I am asking is that the school respect my religious beliefs by not bringing any discussion of homosexuality into my children's classroom.

RACHEL: If you want the school to respect your religious beliefs, then you need to respect the stance we take about teaching about tolerance for others.

> *(All three student teachers and the students from the GSA and STAR applaud. Some of the students whistle)*
>
> *(To ANNE)* I can't believe I said tolerance.

ANNE: Whatever gets the job done.

CHRIS: As a school, I think we have to do more than teach about tolerance. I don't want to be tolerated. I want to be respected for who I am. A gay teenager.

PARENT 2: We live in a world where the person in the next cubicle to you at work could be gay. You don't have to believe in what they do or what they think or say, but you do have to be able to work with them.

> *(There is a pause in the discussion)*

KAREN: *(Looks at her watch)* Well, it's getting late. Can we move on to other business?

> Or are there other comments or questions?

PARENT 1: I have a comment. I call on you, as principal of this school, to prohibit any further discussion of homosexuality during the school day.

PARENT 3: Or at least require permission slips for students to attend the sessions on homosexuality.

RACHEL: *(Angry)* If you want us to send home permission slips to talk about gay and lesbian lives, do you want us to also send home slips to talk about African-Canadian lives or Chinese lives or women's lives? I really have a problem with that, I really do.

ANNE: Your point's well taken. At the same time, as the members of STAR – Students and Teachers Against Racism – will tell you, we still have a long way to go before we can say the school curriculum does a good job of affirming all our students' lives.

KAREN: Well, there's been a lot of food for thought shared here. I want to think carefully about what everyone has said tonight. I also want to undertake an in-depth assessment of what students have learned from this year's Anti-Racism and Pride Week before making any decisions about its future. I'll report the results of the assessment at our next School Council meeting.

PARENT 1: Well, you can be sure my kids won't be attending any of the gay activities.

KAREN: Thank you all for your participation in this discussion. We're going to move on, now, to the next item of business, the Government's Community Service requirement.

End of Play

Discussion Questions About Snakes and Ladders

1. Think about a moment in the play that resonated with your own experience. In what ways, if any, did it resonate with something in your own life or the life of someone you know? If there wasn't a moment in the play that resonated with your own experience, name a moment that surprised you and reflect upon why it was surprising.
2. Think about a moment in the play that provoked an emotional response for you. What was it and why do you think that you responded emotionally to that moment?
3. Which character, if any, in the play did you relate to the most? Why? In what way do you share the privileges and challenges that character faces? In what way are your own privileges and challenges different?
4. Think about a moment in the play that you thought was important for teachers and other educators. What can educators learn from this moment? Relate your analysis to one of the letters in this book.
5. Name three things you are taking away from your reading of Snakes and Ladders.

Notes

1 I want to acknowledge and thank the participants of the research I undertook at the Toronto District School Board from 2002–2003; the Social Sciences and Humanities Research Council of Canada which funded the research; Anthony Collins, Michael Halder, Andria Lepia, Susan Sturma, Anand Mahadevan for research and writing assistance, and the participants in

Debra Chasnoff and Helen Cohen's film *It's Elementary* (Women's Educational Media, 1996). Their perspectives and some of their words also appear in this script. From Cambridge Friends School, a Quaker school in Cambridge, Massachusetts: Thelma Delgado Jossey and Thomas W. Price. From Hawthorne Elementary School, a public school in Madison, Wisconsin: Cecila Klehr and Terri Stron. From Luther Burbank Middle School, a public school in San Francisco, California: Kim Coates. From P.S. 87, a public school in New York City: Scott Hirshfield.

2 In a post-reading discussion, one participant noted that there is a hypervisibility of Rahima's religious beliefs about homosexuality in the play in comparison to John's beliefs about homosexuality. This insight provokes the question of which characters' beliefs, discomfort, conflict, and negotiation have been featured in the play and which characters' have not. It is an important question.

OUT AT SCHOOL

by Tara Goldstein, Jenny Salisbury, and Pam Baer

Scene 1

Putting lipstick on a pig

VICTORIA MASON: I have one daughter. She's 13 years old . . . I also have a partner. We've been together since 2012, and she has two small children, but we don't live in the same household.

When my daughter was 11 . . . I said one day, "You know, I have something to tell you . . ." [I told her I was in a relationship with a woman] and it was really interesting because she just took it . . . my daughter's response was overwhelmingly supportive . . . I can't remember exactly what my daughter said, but it was something like, you know, "This, this is good mommy, we will get through it. If people are mean to you out in the world, we will get through this together. This is great that, you know, that you're kind of being honest about who you are . . ." It seemed, it seemed good at the time.

My daughter's currently enrolled in Grade 8 . . . we're having more challenges as she is getting older . . .

. . . One of our favourite shows is *Grey's Anatomy* . . . and there was one episode this past year where, um, the, the two [women] doctors kissed. And they weren't like making out, it was a (*puckers her lips to show a quick peck of a kiss*) and my daughter was like, "Eeew," and then I was like, "Woah! You know what? You may feel the way you feel" – because I can't legislate her feelings – "but you will not have homophobic reactions in this house!" And so she shut it down.

At my daughter's request I have not come out at school ... But there are other same-sex couples at the school. We're everywhere. As a matter of fact, the administrator of her school is a gay man, um, in a relationship, and, um, they have a son. And that's known ... But, um, I just don't see a lot of action as a school. Um, I think individual teachers will engage in conversations and will work around all kinds of different equity issues. I shouldn't even say that. Um, I don't even think that's true. Teachers reading LGBTQ children's books in the school? Probably not. Inclusion of historical figures in the curriculum? No ... What I see is positive space posters on the wall. I think it does nothing. I think it provides lip service to something that's trending right now and is popular. And it makes us look as if we, it's putting lipstick on a pig. We have the things, the accoutrements of equity on the walls, right? ... They really are decoration without any substance. And I don't see active talk about programming or curriculum, um, I, I, I see posters and lip service ...

... There are things that should be happening more consistently like the honouring of LGBTQ people and their lives, and their families as part of just talking about our world, and who we are, and our normal lives.

Scene 2

Outing my kids

KARLEEN PENDLETON JIMÉNEZ: Looking the way I do, most people presume that I am lesbian. I mean, you could just not say it and have everybody whisper it. I'm just out in every aspect of my life, okay? So, I find it the hardest when I go and pick the kids up, or take them to school. Because then people, the other kids would start, they were just on it right away: Oh, who's that? Oh, well, you know, why does that person look like a boy? You know, how is that person related to your family? And so, um, I felt, like, just picking them up as a butch outed [my kids]. And ... I felt bad about it ... I wanted the power to be out or not to rest within them. And if they wanted to tell about their family, fine, and if they didn't, fine. But if I was picking them up, there was no way to avoid it. And you could tell the kids just start staring at you right away.

I do workshops in schools all the time, from kindergarten to university, and kids stare at me and ask me questions, and that's fine because I'm going there to educate them. And, um, I like that kids are honest, particularly around gender, and I feel like we can get a lot of work done, a lot of learning done, interacting with kids. So I actually really enjoy that. But, with my kids, I couldn't, I couldn't, you know, when I left, I couldn't be there to watch out for them. I don't mind fighting my own battle, but, you know, when you have somebody that you love, and they're smaller and more vulnerable than you, and you can't be there to defend them, it really sucks. That hurts. Probably in all the things that I do, that ['s] the hardest.

Scene 3

So far so good

MARY EVERED: My daughter is enrolled in Grade 7 in a Catholic arts high school.

I have to say, um, it's been fantastic . . . It's always just been very positive. I, I can't think of a single instance where, where it wasn't . . .

When my daughter started at the school, one of the very first things I did was I, I made an appointment to see her religion teacher, [. . .] a wonderful person. Um, so I sat down with her, probably in the third week of September, and, and, um, described our family to her. And, uh, because I know, I've taught Grade 7 religion before, and I know there's a component of it about family life, and human sexuality, and, and all of that kind of thing. And I wanted the teacher to be aware of, uh, the situation, you know, in my daughter's life so that any teaching around family would be inclusive of our family as well, so that my daughter would not feel like, you know, there was something bizarre about her family. [. . .]

So we thought, "Okay, well, here we are pioneers, we will have to do a little extra to make sure we educate them," and it was never a huge amount of trouble. [. . .]

The teacher was very receptive and very open to it. [My daughter] recently had to do a project on, on types of families, and that kind of thing. There was a letter that came home about, that, you know, they

would be discussing different sexualities and family and relational, relationship issues, and that kind of thing, just to get
our permission to proceed. And, you know, my daughter, like a
typical pubescent 12-year-old, was like, "I don't wanna talk
about it! Just sign it! I don't wanna – you know," um, which
was kind of funny. But we noticed that in, in the whole thing
of, of, um, of gender language and that, there was nothing
about transgender people.

So we just penciled that in. And, um, you know, I haven't heard
back from the teacher. I'm sure she, she's the kind of wonderful
person who just, "Oh yeah, I should have done that!"

So we just, you know, it's in those kind of quiet ways that we just,
we just want to keep pushing the envelope.

Scene 4

They wrapped her in the flag

MAY ADDLEY: We are a family of three parents. We call ourselves
polyfidelitious. We have four kids. I'm a part time lunchroom
supervisor. And I volunteer in my son's kindergarten class one day a
week, and then I volunteer in my daughter's Grade 1 class another
day a week. I'm usually at the school at least three or four days a
week. I'm there constantly. And I love it. And, uh, I try to infiltrate
the system with as much positive trans stuff as I possibly can.
Fielding a lot of questions for, for Violet.

Parents have to advocate for their children. Just after my 6-year-
old daughter became Violet, I found out there was the first trans flag
raising at City Hall. So I thought, you know, this is perfect. We need
something fun where we can go and celebrate this! So we got all
fancied up, and we went down, and we saw the flag go up. And we
saw other trans people who were, like, encouraging her. They even
wrapped her in the flag!

We arrived at City Hall and she said, "We're going to a flag
raising, because I'm transgender!" And it was the first time she said it
out loud! And I'm, like, I could feel it coming out, "You don't have
to!" But I didn't, I was just like, "I'm proud of you! . . ." Because it
was, it was great, it was just weird for me. So we did that, and, uh,
you know, we're leaving and she's looking back and she's seeing that

flag that represents her, and she's like, "We should come back tomorrow and see it!"

We met a couple activists at the flag raising, and then we saw things that were going on in the community. Cheri DiNovo was trying to ban conversion therapy with people under the age of 18. So we went for the second reading, and, uh, you know, Violet . . . got to go to Queen's Park and see how people legislate, like as much as she could pay attention. I actually brought all the kids so we could all see what was going on. And then, um, they invited us back for, for the justice committee meeting . . . So I was whispering into Violet's ear, "Okay, this person is this person, and this is what they're saying about this, and this person is opposing it because they think this." And just trying to simply explain it to her. So by the time it was like third reading, she knew what it was, she was passionately against it. She was like, "I hate reparative therapy!" And she's, you know, like really, really, like serious about it.

So, we went and, um, you know, and they were clapping and I was like, "This is the moment" and she was like, "I can't wait until this isn't just Ontario, this is, like, Canada!" So she was thinking, like, beyond herself. And, um, and then, yeah, a reporter showed up and, um, put his mic in her face and he was like, "Why are we here, maybe mom can help you!" And she's like, "Um, I was in the chamber to hear the third reading of Bill-77 to ban conversion therapy for, um, people in Ontario." And he's just like, "Woah! You're six?!" But it's so important to me that she knows why she's there! She's not some puppet.

She was the only kid there representing something that would affect people just like her. And she had to know why. I wanted her to know why. We discussed it on the way there, on the way back. It's a long journey. So when it happened, we just, we squeezed each other's hands because you're not allowed to clap. It was just such a huge deal, and she knew what it meant.

Scene 5

You have to start the work at the beginning

KARLEEN PENDLETON JIMÉNEZ: You have to start the work at the beginning. I say, even the earliest, the earliest thing that happened with [my son] was when he was in, maybe preschool or daycare or whatever they call it. You know, he was four and they did [this chart], you'll see this in the kindergarten curriculum, you know, my, you know, about family, and he had to write my mom's name is blank, my dad's name is blank, my siblings' names are blank. And up until that time, he didn't ever think anything was weird about our family. And then, when he had to fill that out, he just started crying, and he fell apart. He was a wreck, probably for a month, over that, because the little chart didn't match. So, [we went] to the teacher, not angry with her, but just like, "Hey, you know this isn't just a gay issue, like there are many different kinds of families." And she started crying. She was really upset that she had hurt his feelings. But [she] just didn't know, you know? . . .

Scene 6

This is my papa and this is my other papa

MAX REDECOPP: [When I began to transition] . . . I approached them [the school] and I said this is the new reality of our family, and you're going to be hearing different names and different pronouns, different experiences than you may have heard previously. Going forward, this is our family. And if you need more information, I am more than happy to meet . . .

   . . . That first week [there] was a little bit of – few hiccups here and there. But now it's all smoothed over. And my son . . . [was in] junior kindergarten and so I said [to the school], "When you discuss families you are going to hear 'my dads.' You're going to hear, you know, if you ask, 'What about your dad?' they'll probably ask, 'Which one?' And there's going to be language that you may or may not be used to hearing." We're not privy to any other families', you know, [other] families' make-up in terms of orientation or anything like that so I just assumed that, you know, this was the first time they'd ever heard about [having two dads].

   They were so supportive I was just taken aback. I couldn't believe it. I got messages of support from all of the – all of the administration, just saying, "This is fantastic, thank you for letting us know. We are going to be doing as much as we can." In fact, the next day, one of the women at the daycare, and it was like pre- and after-school care, so it was either before or after [school], took all the children and brought them on the mat and started talking about families. And [she] used different dolls, and things, and figures and said, "Show us your family." And when it finally got to [my son] at one point, you know, he was discussing, "This is my papa, and this is my other papa" and then it was just like without a beat, other kids were like, "Oh, you know, I have like two aunts ..." And so it started a conversation and the [woman at the daycare] said that she had never seen children so happy to discuss their families. And it was a very, she even said that it was a safe space and they knew that they didn't have to worry about any judgement. And she – the kids were just like, "Oh that's, really, oh that's great, and what about you, wow, really neat!" So it was really interesting because it opened up a whole new dialogue, I guess that they hadn't done before. But I felt that the way they approached it was just so top notch.

Scene 7

Mother's Day and Father's Day

(SHELBY approaches one microphone, MARY approaches the second microphone, MICHAEL and ERNST share a microphone, showing that they are a family. EVAN and JESS also share a microphone, showing that they are a family.)

SHELBY: Let's talk about Mother's Day and Father's Day. So, that came up because what do schools do? You know, they celebrate these Hallmark moments, and ... kids get to make you something. And so right from the get go, you know, our son had to deal with, well, "I've got two moms." Right? But luckily Mother's Day is in May, so ... the teachers said, "Okay, um, you can either make them both something for Mother's Day, or you can choose to do one now, and one for say Father's Day so you're not left out when the other kids are doing something." And that's how they, right from the beginning, that's what pattern emerged. And every year it was kind of the same thing ... [I]t worked up until Grade 5 ... In Grade 6 he chose not to do something at Father's Day, and I also got a card on Mother's Day.

MARY EVERED: I have a wonderful partner ... and we've been together for 18 years. And, uh, we have a just-turned 12-year-old daughter ... One of the very first things we always did was to meet the teacher on, you know, the curriculum night they have in September and say, "This is [our daughter]'s family." And that, that our expectation was that her family would be treated, in any discussion of families, that we would be a part of it. And, and for the most part, I think that happened. But, you know, there was inevitably some discussion about, you know, how it all worked, and things like, "Oh, it's Father's Day coming up, let's make a Father's Day card!" . . . Her teachers were, were so wonderful when she was so young . . . They said, "Oh, it's Father's Day, oh well, here . . . make, make a card for your granddad." So they dealt with it that way. And they would give her extra time on Mother's Day to make two presents, and two cards . . . So, you know, I'm, I, I'm not really sure how much more we could have expected . . . She was the only child in that situation and they did take some very positive steps to make sure that she was included.

MICHAEL MANCINI: Mother's Day and Fathers' Day was really interesting because, early on, the teachers would feel they were supporting us by having our children make Mothers' Day presents for us. But our daughters have birth mothers and they have a relationship with them.

ERNST HUPEL: We are in touch with their birth mothers. So, early on, [our eldest daughter] would go and say, "My teacher said I don't have a mom, but I do, her name is Heather." So, you know, the teachers were doing it to actually support us. But after [both our daughters] said, "No, I actually have a mother" . . . they began to make Mothers' Day cards for their birth mothers and we send the cards to them and, yeah, so . . . We get double Fathers' Day cards.

MICHAEL MANCINI: It's a big day.

ERNST HUPEL: It is! It's like Christmas here.

JESS SWANCE-SMITH: [Teachers shouldn't] assume what a child's family may look like . . . take their word for it. I mean if they say they have multiple people in their family, let them make those, you know, ten Mother's Day cards that they need to make. (*Evan and Jess laugh*). Or whatever, five Father's Day cards because maybe there's, you know, . . . maybe an aunt or an uncle who's like a father or a mother to them.

EVAN SMITH: I think one thing I really appreciate is that, for instance, at Mother's Day, the school wasn't sure who identified, you know, as a mother, for sure, and so they just sent out like, you know, a blanket message through our, you know, we have, like, an app we use to communicate with teachers and they sent out a message saying, you know, "We need to know who in your family identifies as a mother and should be getting a Mother's Day card."

Scene 8

When it's unsafe for trans kids to be out

DAWN: Kids are smart, they really pick up on the cues from the adults, like some kids, especially if their parents don't support them, they will change themselves if they pick up any kind of cues from the adults that the adults aren't comfortable. So the kid will think, "Well, this adult's not comfortable with me being trans, so I'll just present as cisgender to this person." They can tell who is a safe person and who isn't a safe person a lot quicker than you realize. So you may have lost your chance if you don't – if you create an unsafe space.

There are a lot of things that people do without realizing that they're doing it that make it unsafe for trans kids to come out. Like … the language that you use, like saying boys or girls instead of kids or children. And dividing the class, like boys over here, girls over here. Because that happened to my child. I was on a field trip and it's like, "Okay, boys line up here and girls line up here" and then my child was, like, literally standing in between the two lines with this frantic look, and then stood in the girls' line … This was the first year of her transition, when she was only six, and everyone kinda laughed, like they didn't laugh at her, but they laughed thinking that she was just being funny. But I think that's a difficult situation because not everybody identifies as a boy or a girl, so divide people in groups in different ways … Also talk about these things, have the books in the classroom … Somebody may feel safe talking to you if you make a safe environment.

Scene 9

In high school it's a little bit harder

DALE ATLAS JONES: Hello. My name is Dale and, uh, I have two mothers and a biological father who is also gay. Right now, I'm going to Westside Collegiate Institute. And I'm in the IB program there. The international baccalaureate program. Yeah, it's a program that's international, so it's the same throughout the world. So if you're doing IB in England, it'll be the same as in Canada.

I've never felt a fear or discomfort talking about my family. I usually find it very easy to talk about my family, but it's not something that I, uh, I talk about without any social cues. If we're talking about family at home and if they bring up a dad who isn't really, "I don't really have a dad that I live with full time." Or sometimes if there's people who are a little bit, if they're homophobic, I bring up that I come from an LGBTQ family. It usually, um, surprises kids who don't expect it to come from me, and I've never had much backlash from doing it because most of the time the community isn't very accepting of, like, bullying, when it comes to homophobia or other topics.

In elementary school they were a little bit more accepting, I think. In high school it's a little bit harder to, I find, to be accepting of, because kids become a lot more confident, and that means that bullies become a lot more confident, and it's harder when it comes to homophobia. It is stronger as you go up through the grades . . .

There's never been too much LGBTQ curriculum taught. It has come up with teachers who have identified as gay or lesbian, but it's never been taught or talked about unless there's an issue that comes up that needs to be addressed, in which case it is always addressed. But there's nothing that is in the curriculum that talks about the LGBTQ community.

Scene 10

Changing the world

KARLEEN PENDLETON JIMÉNEZ: I think probably the hardest, uh, go we had of it was with our 17-year-old daughter, who, it seemed like, had to be in charge of the social justice work at her elementary school, and then middle school, and then high school, you know? I'd say maybe the first three or four years it wasn't a big issue. By Grade 4, people were outwardly saying a lot of homophobic things, especially if they knew she had two moms. And she pretty much ran her own campaign, and, um, educated the teachers.

(Chuckles)

[My daughter] has published a piece [about something that happened when] she was in Grade 4. They were reading a Reader's Digest version of Shakespeare and, it was *Twelfth Night*, when two of the characters that were in theory women – anyway, you know,

Shakespeare messes it all up. Anyway, so they were all about to kiss and then this other kid went "Eeeew," you know, "Eeeew, they're lesbos," and my daughter said, "Shut up!" She just shouted at the girl, "Shut up!" The teacher asked her to leave the room to calm down. And she didn't say she was in trouble, but, you know, being asked to leave the room feels like you are in trouble. I think the teacher felt bad. They haven't received any education about [how to handle] this . . .

. . . In high school, she's had a much better time. In Grade 9 she co-founded a [Gay Straight Alliance club] at her school and enlisted all of her friends to be a part of it. She's used the GSA [club] as a mechanism to make it a lot more queer friendly at her school. Poster campaigns, and everything. And you know, as soon as they put up the posters, they tear them down. Right, you just put them back up again! They've been doing that for four years, and, and tons of kids have been involved, and they're so political. And I've gone to speak with them too. And they're lovely, you know, they're just like . . . these young activists that have been pushed and like, "WOW, what are we doing?" I said, you know, at the time when I spoke to them I said, "The biggest activist work I did in high school was lead a campaign against a band director who I thought was an asshole, and you're like changing the world."

Scene 11

There has to be some intentionality

VICTORIA MASON: You know, it shouldn't be the responsibility of our children to set up [Gay Straight Alliances] and do the work for the teachers. And we can't depend on individual wonderful teachers who still have to send home permission slips to talk about us. We really need to create a space where LGBTQ people and families are normalized . . . *(With increasing passion)* That means that it's talked about. It's not that thing that we don't talk about . . . It's part of the curriculum, it's part of the fabric of, of the school, just like the straight families are. You know what I mean? . . . I think there has to be some intentionality.

Index